WHEN
FEAR
SPEAKS...
LISTEN

The Seven Messengers of Fear

By
Dennis Merritt Jones, DD

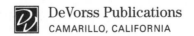

DeVorss Publications
CAMARILLO, CALIFORNIA

WHEN FEAR SPEAKS LISTEN
Copyright © 2024
by Dennis Merritt Jones

Print ISBN: 9780875169514
ebook ISBN: 9780875169521

Library of Congress Catalog Card Number: 2024931410

This publication is offered with the understanding that the publisher and
author are not giving psychological, medical, financial, legal, or other
professional advice. If such assistance is needed by the reader, please seek
the services of a licensed professional.

First Printing, 2024

DeVorss & Company, Publisher
P.O. Box 1389
Camarillo CA 93011-1389
www.devorss.com
Printed in the United States of America

Library of Congress Cataloging-in-Publication Data

Names: Jones, Dennis Merritt, author.
Title: When Fear Speaks: The 7 Messgners of Fear / by Dennis Merritt Jones.
Description: First DeVorss Publications Edition. | Camarillo, California:
DeVorss Publications, 2024. | Summary: When Fear Speaks, Listen will help you
understand what your fears are telling you, how to move beyond them and experi-
ence the joy of life.
- Provided by publisher.
Identifiers: LCCN 2024931410 (print) | LCCN 2024931411 (ebook) | ISBN
9780875169514 (trade paperback) | ISBN 9780875169521 (ebook)
Subjects: LCSH: Mind and body. | Psychology. | Self-Help.
Classification: LCC BF161 .C146 2024 (print) | LCC BF161 (ebook) | DDC 128/.2–
dc23/eng/20221212
LC record available at https://lccn.loc.gov/ 2024931410
LC ebook record available at https://lccn.l0c.gov/2024931411

"This book is a masterpiece, an impressive example of taking an unpleasant emotion prevalent in the world today and refining an interpretation of Its meaning to the extent that it becomes a guiding light on our human journey and not an unpleasant emotion that needs to be defeated. I believe *When Fear Speaks ... Listen* is a must-read that will enhance human experiences."

— **ANGELO PIZELO**, Emerson Theological Inst.

"Dennis Merritt Jones has created a masterful treatise for healing fear! As a facilitator of voice dialogue for 40 years, I find his brilliant method of dialoguing with each of the "Seven Messengers of Fear" to be the most integrative treatment I've experienced on the subject."

— **PATRICK J. HARBULA D.D.**, Best-selling author of *The Magic of the Soul*

"Sometimes, someone delivers an idea that is ripe for the age. Dennis Merritt Jones has delivered again. *When Fear Speaks . . . Listen,* captures the time and the pulse of living in balance with the anxiety of the age--the individual's desire to live in harmony. So.... if you are struggling with reconciling your feelings of dread with your practice of inner peace, this is the book for you."

— **DR. KENN GORDON**, Past Spiritual Leader of Centers for Spiritual Living

"I wholeheartedly recommend Dennis Merritt Jones' newest book, *When Fear Speaks . . . Listen* to anyone who seeks to transcend the limitations of fear and embrace the fullness of their being."

— **ELIZABETH CANTEY**, author of *Living Enlightened—The Joy of Integrating Spirit, Mind and Body.*

"I have had the privilege of being a colleague and friend of Dennis Merritt Jones for over thirty years. He is a master teacher. *When Fear Speaks . . . Listen* is most needed for our times and I know for sure you will be changed at depth."

— **TEMPLE HAYES**, Author and New Thought Leader

"We have all dealt with fear on some level and *When Fear Speaks . . . Listen* is a beautiful guidebook to teach how to deal with these powerful messengers and actually transform."

— **CYNTHIA JAMES**, Best-selling Author, International Speaker, and Coach

"*When Fear Speaks . . . Listen* may cause you to feel uncomfortable at times. It will likely make you laugh as well. And, it will definitely inspire you to think and grow. Dr. Dennis Merritt Jones has once again invited us to come to the edge..."

— **REV. STEPHANIE SORENSON**, Author of *The Sacred Continuum*

"Few people are philosophers. Dennis Merritt Jones has spent the majority of his waking hours immersed in both the purpose of life, learning from everything that happens to us, and surrendering to our highest and best self. Dr. D is in the truest sense a philosopher of life. *When Fear Speaks ... Listen* invites us to confront and learn from what we usually avoid. Transcending fear is the next journey in human evolution!"

— **DR. CHERIE CARTER-SCOTT**, NY Times best-selling author of *If Life Is a Game, Here Are the Rules*

"A captivating and empowering book that leads the reader to a life of courage and peace from within. Expert guidance to unlocking your true potential. I will be giving my patients copies for years to come."

— **MICHELLE BRIGGS**, PMHNP-BC (Psychiatric mental health nurse practitioner- board certified)

"I feel so strongly about Dennis Merritt Jones 'approach to life that we have shared his wisdom in our community news magazine 10 times a year for almost a decade."

— **PETER ROOS**, Publisher and Editor of *Paradise News*

"As a career corporate trainer, I have witnessed how Fear significantly impacts the behavior of professionals, particularly in sales. Fear impacts decision-making, interpersonal relationships, and quality of life. *When Fear Speaks ... Listen* will help you master Fear in your life."

— **MIKE BOSWORTH**, Best Selling Author/Speaker/Sales

"Like physical pain, we may not want to feel fear, but it is an ally — a valuable symptom. In *When Fear Speaks . . . Listen*, Dennis Merritt Jones helps us face it and explore it, to understand the profound intuitive wisdom Fear offers the brave seeker."

— **MICHAEL BENNER**, Radio host and author of *Fearless Intelligence*

"This timely, and beautifully written book by Dennis Merritt Jones, will help you turn fear into one of your greatest teachers. *When Fear Speaks...Listen* is much needed today as we face unprecedented challenges that ignite fear in us more than ever before."

— **ORA NADRICH**, Author of *Time to Awaken: Changing the World with Conscious Awareness*

"In *When Fear Speaks ... Listen,* Dennis Merritt Jones brings his inspirational voice to one of the greatest obstacles to personal growth, fear. Accompany him on this journey of personal realization and watch your experience of life improve."

— **JIM LOCKARD**, author of *Creating the Beloved Community* and *Being the Beloved Community*

"On the other side of your greatest Fears lies a life of freedom, authentic power, and inner peace. With a style of writing that is clear and a structure that is creative and informative, *When Fear Speaks. . . Listen* will take you there."

— **REV. WENDY CRAIG-PURCELL**, Spiritual Leader, The Unity Center

TABLE OF CONTENTS

Introduction

Occasionally, someone will ask me upon what source of information I base my ideas, themes, logic, and opinions as a writer. Some will ask if I am a therapist or a psychologist, and my reply is, "No, I am neither. I am an ontologist and New Thought theologist and have been for over forty years." In metaphysics, an ontologist is one who delves into the nature of being, existence, and reality to find relevance, purpose, and meaning with the life he or she is shaping today. Philosophical questions such as, "Why are we here? Where did we come from?" and "What is ours to do, and what keeps us from doing it?" are wonderful fodder for meaningful conversation.

A New Thought theologist, on the other hand, studies the nature of God (or whatever name we wish to assign to that "Something" that is larger than ourselves). We seek to understand and experience our oneness with the omnipresence, omniscience, and omnipotence of a spiritual Universe. Finding the relevance and inclusion of spirituality (rather than religiosity) in our lives is a daily practice that keeps us moving forward on a journey to a place we never left, i.e., our oneness with Life. Questions such as, "What role does my awareness of God's presence play in my life today?" and "How does it affect my being who I came here to be?" are rich with potential for in-depth, life-changing conversations.

Balancing Doing with Being

What I have discovered is that by commingling ontology and New Thought theology, I get the best of both worlds. It's how we balance and merge our *being* nature with our *doing* nature that matters. My theme song could be "Do, Be, Do, Be, Do." One without the other creates imbalance. This is what makes us whole human beings, finding the balance between our inner world of being and our outer world of doing. The result is a sense of wholeness that supersedes all conditions.

As you read *When Fear Speaks...Listen*, you'll discover the line between the two worlds is extremely thin, which is why, when, where, and how Fear sneaks through the back door of our minds and raises its gnarly head.

Seeking purpose and meaning in life and developing an awareness of our oneness with our Higher Power seem to go hand-in-hand when creating a life worth living. It also seems that Fear is only too happy to accompany us on the journey, trying as it may to impede our forward progress. That's just the way Fear operates. Its mission is to create as many diversions along the way as it can. Anytime we step up and out of the trenches and make a move toward a better life, Fear and its messengers will all do their best to ambush us and slow us down. But why is that? We seldom stop and ask that question.

Perhaps Fear has ulterior motives for being in our lives that we have yet to discover. Thus, the purpose of this book is to better understand Fear's motivation, purpose, and reason for involving itself in both our being and our doing. As you'll learn, the endgame is worth the read. Fear has a message that is tailored just for us, and we need to listen carefully.

I am honored that you have joined me on this journey. Onward and upward!

Peace,

Dennis Merritt Jones

This book is dedicated to you, the reader, already on the Journey of Awakening to your true Power. Irrespective of who you are, where you are, your station in life, your history, or what the future may presumably hold for you, know that you are never alone. Within you lies a Power that can transcend even your greatest Fears.

Be still…listen, and know.

It is as old as time itself.

Its presence can motivate us, most often out of desperation rather than inspiration.

It can cause us to shift our gaze and shirk back into a darkened corner to hide rather than look into its steely eyes.

It moves many people to think, say, and do regretful things.

It is also difficult to identify because it wears so many deceiving disguises.

In addition, it causes us to react rather than respond to what arises in the moment.

"It" is Fear, and most of us try to avoid it like the plague.

Perhaps there's a better way to deal with our fears, by mindfully listening to what they have to say...

PART ONE

• • • • • • •

The Energy of Fear

Welcome to a Most Unusual Exploration

Wisdom says that the better we understand something,
the more logically we will be able to deal with it.
We might best understand the anatomy of fear
by first dissecting it and seeing it for what
it is and what it is not.

DENNIS MERRITT JONES
The Art of Uncertainty

Fear is a topic that, well, scares the pants off most of us. After all, that is why we are intrigued by Fear. We want to know more about how it works and why it seems to dominate so much bandwidth in our daily lives. Perhaps, more than any other reason, you have joined me on this journey because we all would like to know how to mitigate Fear and take back some of the power we have given it for most of our lives.

This is a worthy pursuit that will enrich not only our lives, but the world in general. Metaphysically speaking, there is only one of us here, so when we can personally transcend the bondage of Fear, the world becomes a better place for us all.

The primal energy of Fear has been the root cause of every war ever fought and every act of violence, selfishness, and greed visited upon humankind. It has created more collective suffering than any other single thing. It's as if Fear took on a life of its own since the beginning of time, and it has been on a mission ever since to invade every aspect of our lives and leave us feeling helpless, alone, and powerless. For millennia, Fear has sponsored the false bravado that motivates despots and bullies, while others timidly withdraw into the shadows of their own Fear. It has been used to manipulate and control the masses and weaken our resolve to take a stand. There is not (nor has there ever been) a single human being or sentient creature on the planet who has not, at some point, known the debilitating effects of Fear. It rages through our mind and body, triggering the fight-or-flight reaction. And, all too often we buckle under and mindlessly run from it, if not literally, then metaphorically.

Have you ever heard this acronym for FEAR: "**F**orget **E**verything **A**nd **R**un"? Too often that is what we do when Fear arises. We tend to turn as quickly as possible from it. In denial, thinking we can outrun it, we head to the medicine cabinet, liquor cabinet, refrigerator, shopping mall, or some other form of behavior that offers a temporary escape. The only problem with temporary escapes is that they are exactly that...tempo-

4

rary. At some point we must return to reality, and when we do the same Fear is there waiting to pick up where it left off.

Why is it that when Fear of any kind ascends from within, we'll do just about anything to avoid it rather than stop, turn, face it, and ask what business it has interfering with our life at that particular moment? In the midst of running, *that* idea seldom occurs. However, if we were willing to stand toe-to-toe with our Fear, we might be surprised at what it has to share with us.

Perhaps we need to assign a new meaning to the acronym F.E.A.R. We seldom want to do that because, well, we're too scared to think clearly.

When we are deeply frightened, our reptilian brain kicks in, provoking us to mindlessly *react* rather than mindfully *respond* to the thoughts and emotions that stimulate Fear. We've been conditioned to run from Fear, and, in the process, we unknowingly give it another free pass to do with us as it pleases. It's as if we have created a space, a home, in our minds and hearts and given Fear a master key to come and go at will. That's what Fear does. It comes and goes, and comes and goes, as it has done for the past 300 millennia. And, it will continue to do so unless WE do something differently. It seldom occurs to us that we are active participants in this ancient game of hide-and-seek we play with Fear. We have a choice in the matter. Unmitigated Fear can be a bully, and like all bullies it needs to be faced down, called out, and revealed for what it is.

Instead of running from Fear, we need to confidently stand up to it, listen to it, and face it straight on. The new acronym for FEAR?

Face **E**verything **A**nd **R**ethink.

If we are willing to **F**ace **E**verything **A**nd **R**ethink, the endgame might surprise us. This book is designed to shed new light on Fear to enable us to "see" it and thus experience it in a new way. Wisdom tells us we can't outrun Fear because it simply morphs, shape-shifts, and changes its appearance to fit the occasion. We can't outrun Fear because it knows exactly where we are going and rushes ahead to meet us there. It is able to tailor itself to reflect our deepest concerns regarding loss.

To accomplish this, Fear has created numerous disguises, each a messenger to represent it.

The Seven Messengers of Fear

While the faces of Fear are legion, in the context of this book the seven most prevalent disguises that Fear hides behind are:

Anger, Worry, Judgement, Selfishness, Shame, Loneliness, and Uncertainty.

Each of these messengers of Fear bring along a host of other descendants. While some people may not see these seven messengers as Fear in disguise, that is precisely what they are. Once we elevate our perspective and refocus our perception of Fear, we'll be able to see it for what it really is... *and isn't.*

Perhaps it's time to give Fear a new identity, to break it down piece by piece and examine it. For eons, humans have perceived Fear as a brutal enemy, a merciless opponent to fight, avoid, negotiate with, or try to outrun. With this mindset, our innate response to Fear often pours gasoline on the fire, generating more Fear, which only exacerbates the problem—fueling, re-energizing, and enlarging the very thing we are running from. It's not a stretch of the imagination to say that Fear is the single most misunderstood impulse of energy in the human condition. With Mindfulness, courage, and clear intention, that can change. When we learn to listen to the Seven Messengers of Fear proactively, we can transcend the reactive reptilian brain, which then allows us to ...

... **F**ace **E**verything **A**nd **R**ethink!

Our Perspective and Perception of Fear Matters

Nothing in life is to be feared; it is only to be understood. Now is the time to understand more so that we may fear less.

MARIE CURIE

Perspective and Perception are two different things, and both need to be acknowledged, understood, and brought into play when dealing with the messengers of Fear when they come knocking on our door...and they will. Perspective establishes the height, position, angle, or mindset through which we see something. Perception is the filter that determines what we see and how we interpret it. (We will deeply explore both concepts in the following chapters.)

Fear can dominate our lives in countless ways because we have failed to learn how to interpret its true intentions. What if we could rethink our Fears and view them through another lens of Perception? When we can be mindful of the altitude of our attitude about Fear, our perspective changes and we perceive things differently. What if we could make peace with our Fears and invite them to join our allied forces on a mission to create an amazing life? What if our Fears are actually messengers sent to assist us in successfully making it through life, one day at a time—intact, healthy, and whole—

arriving at the finish line called "a life worth living"? Sounds sort of like fairy-tale thinking, right? Maybe not, but it beckons a new Perspective and Perception that includes courage, faith, trust, and action.

Fear is not our enemy. It is a messenger sent to get our attention and then guide and guard us to keep us alive and safe. The problem is, with our lack of this Perspective, we give Fear a free rein and let it run off with us...terrified. When Fear gets on a roll and takes its job far too seriously, it overwhelms us and holds us hostage in a prison of our own making.

Every Fear bears important information regarding our destiny and future. Learning how to establish healthy boundaries around our Fears can help us proactively discern and receive their messages.

What Can We Learn from Fear?

The question shouldn't be, "How can we rid ourselves of all Fear?" because not only is that a literal impossibility, it's a bad idea. The real question is, "How can we learn to use Fear as a springboard to transcend its crippling energy rather than mindlessly pushing against it or running from it, ultimately giving it more power over us?" We can run, but we can't hide from Fear, nor should we try because it's not real and has no life of its own, other than the life we give it. It's quite amazing how much power we give to something that doesn't really exist until we breathe the breath of life into it.

Fear is an *idea* about something, first birthed in the mind and instantly imbued in the body, skewed by a specific mental and emotional predisposition, perspective, and perception. No one can point to Fear and say, "There it is." However, we can point to the things "out there" that stimulate the invisible energy of Fear, causing it to arise *from within*. This is why Emotional Awareness is so important. It's like an early warning system alerting us to what is percolating in the mind before it boils over. Practicing Emotional Awareness offers us an opportunity to **F**ace **E**verything **A**nd **R**ethink how we will *respond* rather than *react*.

Whence Does Fear Originate?

Every Fear originates from the same place within, where an attachment to a concern of death or loss dominates our attention and reigns supreme. It might be our own physical death we fear or the Fear of losing a loved one, but it could as easily be the death (or loss) of a lifestyle, relationship, career, bank account, possessions, reputation, or health status. The concern about the loss of our personal power related to any of the aforementioned issues often drives many of our Fears. The antithesis of death is life, and life is eternally unfolding in us, through us, and *as us*.

Finding the balance and connection between life and death is not something that happens only at the end of our stay here on the planet. It is a daily practice that invites us to understand and embrace the challenges each day of the journey brings, beginning with the Fears that hold us back, keeping us from living the life we have been sent here to experience with ebullience and awe.

This is why we must **F**ace **E**verything **A**nd **R**ethink. When we understand what our messengers of Fear are telling us, a new life of health and prosperity comes into focus.

Remembering the "Something" That is Bigger Than Our Fear

It's easy to say that the message our every Fear bears is attached to a concern of death or loss of some sort. But, what good does that wisdom do us unless we can internalize it and intentionally apply it in our lives *today* in a manner that alters the trajectory of our destiny *tomorrow*? With Mindfulness, we can find the resolution to meet and transcend Fear by openly receiving the messenger with faith, trusting and knowing we are one with something greater, something bigger than ourselves and our Fear. That with which we are one is known by many different names: Life, Infinite Intelligence, One Power, Universe, Creator, God, It, Omniscience, the Self, Divine Presence, the Beloved, or

11

as some put it, the Source of All That Is. While we'll find many of the aforementioned names in this book, it really doesn't matter what name we use to describe this "Something Bigger." As my friend, Daniel Nahmod, infers in his song "One Power," the only thing that matters is that we understand our relationship and oneness with It, as well as our accessibility to It.

> *Call it God, call it Spirit*
> *Call it Jesus, call it Lord,*
> *Call it Buddha, Bahá 'u 'lláh,*
> *Angel's Wings or Heaven's Door.*
> *But whatever name you give it*
> *It's all One Power, can't you see*
> *It's the power of the love in you and me.*

DANIEL NAHMOD, *"One Power"*

The key is not to overcomplicate the concept with religiosity. In the words of Joseph Campbell, "God is a metaphor for that which transcends all levels of intellectual thought. It's as simple as that." The spiritual reality is that Infinite Intelligence put us here to serve as the open vessels through which It flows into ever-expanding and creative expressions of Itself. It doesn't get much simpler than that. There is an orderliness and beneficence to life that flows in us and through us with simplicity when we faithfully align with the eternal Source of All That Is.

This is where and when a mindful shift in both Perspective and Perception are necessary. Elevating the altitude of our attitude alters our perspective. Things change with a belief that beyond what we Fear lies a Power greater than ourselves. As our Perspective changes, we see things differently. With a new Perception, a new way opens to navigate past, over, under, around, or through whatever the messengers of Fear and their many descendants represent. It is in our oneness with that "Something" bigger than ourselves that we find a resolution to transcending our Fear. However, the agreement with our messengers is that we must first be willing and able to see, hear, feel, and embrace the wisdom they bring. This doesn't mean that after the messenger delivers its message it fades into the ethers and disappears forever. It means that we perceive the Fear differently, faithfully through fresh eyes. It means we have defanged the many-headed beast. With a mind and heart that understand the difference between reacting and responding to Fear, we restore our ability to take back our power.

The Takeaway: Don't Avoid the Messenger!

Making friends with our Fears is the first step in transcending them. This doesn't mean we have to become bosom buddies and constantly hang out with them. It means we must learn to lean in, stand toe-to-toe, and dance with our messengers of Fear, listening to and learning from our master teachers of the moment.

As we already know, too often when Fear overwhelms us, we react by attempting to ban the messenger, or at least avoiding, denying, anesthetizing, invalidating, or pretending we don't hear or see it. It's not about banishing or numbing our Fears. It's about learning to identify, embrace, interpret, and apply the messages they bring, thus essentially making our Fears our allies. Only then can we proactively receive, honor, and disengage with the messengers of Fear and transcend them.

It's important to acknowledge and embrace the fact that our Fears will never go away. They're not supposed to, because when seen clearly and proactively, they become gifts of awakening—gifts meant to enhance our time on the planet, empower us, and shape a life of purpose, meaning, substance, and joy. In some Eastern teachings, they say that we must learn to dance with our demons if we are to understand why they are present in our lives. Getting comfortable with that which we fear requires being teachable by coming closer to it and listening to what it has to say. We can learn to mitigate our Fear and regain our power once we first understand its message. Learning how to thrive and dance with Fear is the practice of a lifetime. However, to do so we must embrace it and become its willing student until we're able to lead the dance. When Fear speaks, it is a mark of wisdom to face it and listen, and it begins by not avoiding the messenger.

Before we talk about each messenger, it's important to understand the formatting and flow of this book.

When Fear Speaks...Listen is formatted in a manner that will enable us to engage with our Fears in a proactive way and learn from them. In each of the following seven chapters we will be introduced to one of Fear's most popular messengers, as well as its closest descendants from the same bloodline.

THE INTERVIEW: Each chapter will feature an exclusive interview with a different messenger of Fear, offering insights on who they are and the agenda with which they come.

THE GOOD NEWS AND THE NOT-SO-GOOD NEWS: There will also be some "Good News" and "Not-So-Good News" about each messenger of Fear. This section is meant to give us insights into both sides of the discussion, allowing us to seek and find the balance required to maintain equanimity and remain teachable.

THE MINDFULNESS PRACTICE: Included at the end of each chapter will be a Mindfulness Practice designed to "put wheels" on each messenger's message through an experiential process that enhances our ability to embody and apply the lesson in real-time. As previously stated: "Realization without application is hallucination."

THE AFFIRMATION: Finally, to close each chapter, an affirmation is offered that is meant to "seal the deal" with each messenger of Fear, affirming the lesson learned. It is encouraged that only one chapter is read in each sitting, allowing ourselves time to receive, listen to, and learn from each messenger.

Are We Ready to Learn How to Dance with Our Messengers?

For an awakened mind, sometimes it's difficult to invite each messenger of Fear onto the dance floor because we're so used to seeing them appear out of nowhere in different settings. In a strange way, some of our Fears may seem like longtime family members with whom we're so close that taking time to embrace and dance with them feels odd and perhaps uncomfortable. However, if we are going to identify and transcend them, it's important to show up at the dance with a positive and affirmative mindset, willing to lead the dance and listen. The practice of Mindfulness will show the way.

Mindfulness Practice

In the following chapters, we shall dive into and examine the many disguises our messengers of Fear wear. This also includes their "descendants," i.e., Fears that sometimes seem so innocuous that they fly under the radar of our discernment. But, they are equally bringing their "A game" to the dance while wearing their own unique disguises. For now, consider the following Mindfulness practice as your first dance lesson.

- Sitting quietly with your eyes closed, visualize yourself in a large group at a dinner party or dance. This is a safe environment in which to be.

- Imagine that sitting in all the chairs are some of your greatest Fears. They are each patiently waiting for you to approach and invite them to start a conversation or move onto the dance floor.

- Now take a moment to gaze around the room and see the messengers of Fear who have shown up for you, each eager and ready to share exactly what you need to know in order to move past them.

- Which Fear is it you most want to avoid? Look at it across the room, but don't stare or flinch. This is important because that is the messenger most eager to share what it knows with you.

17

- For now, just take a deep breath, open your eyes, and smile, knowing you have broken the ice with that messenger. Simply by making eye contact with it, you have introduced your intention to listen and transcend it. Feels good, doesn't it?

As you read the following chapters, realize that each messenger of Fear brings new information, enabling you to understand and transcend it. In this process, you will experience freedom in ways you may never have imagined possible.

AFFIRMATION

"As I venture forward, I am ready, willing, and able to listen to my messengers of Fear, knowing that I receive exactly what I need to know when I need to know it. The windows of my mind and heart are open wide as new wisdom floods in, and I am free."

• • • • • • •

PART TWO

The
Seven Messengers of Fear
and Their Descendants

Anger

The First Messenger of Fear

If you try to get rid of fear and anger without knowing their meaning, they will grow stronger and return.

DEEPAK CHOPRA

Once upon a time, a big, gruff, tough, and battle-hardened samurai warrior went to see a little meek monk. "Monk!" he barked in an angry voice accustomed to instant obedience. "Teach me about heaven and hell!"

The monk slowly looked up at the mighty warrior and replied with utter disdain, "Teach you about heaven and hell? I couldn't teach you about anything. Look at you. You're dumb. You're dirty. You smell bad. Your mother is probably as ugly as you. You're a disgrace, an embarrassment to the samurai class. Get out of my sight. I can't stand you."

The samurai got furious. As his anger grew, he shook and became red in the face, speechless as he trembled with rage. He drew his sword and prepared to slay the monk. Looking directly into the samurai's eyes with great compassion, the monk calmly said, "That's hell."

The samurai froze in place, instantly realizing the compassion and wisdom of the monk who had risked his life to show him hell! He dropped his sword and silently fell to his knees. As the anger and rage drained from his body, the samurai began to weep. Filled with appreciation and humility, he surrendered and collapsed into the monk's open and loving arms. The monk said softly, "And that's heaven."

The story is a classic Zen teaching parable that has been embellished to serve as an illustration of how, when identified and understood, the energy of Anger can be instantly transformed into the peace that passes all understanding. The metaphor is crystal clear: The angry samurai symbolizes a Fear-driven egoic sense of separation from our authentic power, and the compassionate monk symbolizes a love-awakened awareness of our oneness with our authentic power. Do we identify more with the samurai or monk in our story? Anger and Rage arise from a hellish state of mind. Inner Peace and Equanimity arise from a heavenly state of mind. In the context of this chapter, heaven and hell are not physical locations but points of awareness. In other words, the doors of heaven or hell are only one thought away, and we hold the key to both. In which state of mind would we rather exist? In either case, the messenger of Anger has some wisdom to share with us that may help guide our choice.

Transcending our Fears of every nature begins with three necessary requirements: Curiosity, Inquisitiveness, *and* Being Teachable. As angry as he was, our samurai in the story nonetheless met these requirements. Curiosity opens the door to explore new ways of creating a life worth living that we may have never considered. Inquisitiveness invites us to drill down, to query or ask questions about what beckons us to enter that door. Being Teachable is how we discover the reward found in the first two requirements by embracing and applying, with an open mind, that which we learn. As we begin to **F**ace **E**verything **A**nd **R**ethink our quest, may we do so with great Curiosity, courageous query, and an open, teachable mind.

The Descendants of Anger: Rage & Resentment

If we ask and listen mindfully to this messenger of Fear, it will help us understand its message and how to mitigate the problem. The danger of unacknowledged, unmanaged, or suppressed Anger is doubly dangerous when we consider that its direct descendants, Rage and Resentment, are eager and ready to join the party. Interestingly, they do so by moving in diametrically opposed directions. Rage violently surges outward, while Resentment passively submerges inward. Both of these descendants of Anger are equally destructive.

Rage: Rage is a secondary emotion stemming from Anger. Rage is Anger off the hook. It's Anger on steroids, and it can do serious damage to the lives and property of others and ourselves, e.g., road rage. We target the energy of Rage outward *toward* the world and those in it. It's impossible to fly into Rage without first passing through the gates of Anger, one of Fear's greatest facades. As Will Rogers reminded us, "People who fly into a rage always make a bad landing." This is why Emotional Awareness is essential and why, with the right Perspective, it's one gift our messengers of Fear offer us. If we are mindful enough to perceive *and feel* Rage ascending, we can preemptively quell it before the missiles fire at unaware targets.

Resentment: Resentment, another secondary emotion, is also a descendant of Anger. However, Resentment is Anger inverted and turned inward, wherein its corrosive damage can slowly occur before it is discovered and released. Author Ann Carol pointed this out when she wrote, "Resentment is the most potent poison generated in the human body. It causes physical and spiritual wreckage if allowed to boil within." Unresolved repressed Anger, also known as Resentment, can turn our mind and body into a boiler room where Anger's energy slowly brews and becomes more and more toxic over time. Most people who carry deep, prolonged Resentment are not aware that it covertly triggers the "fight-or-flight" response that, when internalized, can lead to potential hormonal changes affecting the heart, blood pressure, and immune system. It can also exacerbate the risk of diabetes, depression, insomnia, and heart disease. Resentment is an invisible killer because it literally and unknowingly "re-sends" the toxins of Fear, disguised as Anger, coursing throughout the entire body in a continuous loop. Again, Emotional Awareness matters to our longevity and well-being.

Interview with Anger

DMJ: Most people don't think of Anger as Fear in one of its scariest disguises. Like the samurai in our story, do you enjoy frightening people? And, if so, what is the payoff for you?

> **ANGER:** *I love scaring people because it gives me the sense of power and control I need to feel safe and prove I am right. There's great power in being right. Frightening people is a wonderful way to intimidate, manipulate, and control them. AND to get what I want, which is more power. That's my jam!*

DMJ: Why do you always act so arrogant, confident, and self-righteous when you express yourself? Who are you trying to impress?

> **ANGER:** *My angry act got your attention, right? When I can terrify and frighten everyone, I have their attention.*

The more attention I get, the more power I get. Therefore, I am on a mission to scare and intimidate whoever threatens me and my sense of power.

DMJ: When you say "whoever threatens you and your sense of power," can you tell me more about that? What or who threatens your sense of power and triggers your reaction most quickly, and how do you express it?

ANGER: *I rise in your mind and body when I feel threatened by something someone says or does that challenges me and my need for power, approval, and love. When I feel threatened, I feel a loss of control. Because I feel powerless in the first place, the threat of the loss of anything that represents external power qualifies for an angry rant.*

DMJ: I have heard that one of your classic go-to moves to impose yourself covertly on others is by acting passive-aggressively toward them. It's sort of an angry sneak attack because there are no fireworks, only bone-chilling silence. Some might refer to it as giving those you are trying to manipulate the silent treatment or cold shoulder. Could you tell me, how and why does that seem to work?

ANGER: *Seriously? Giving someone the silent treatment is gold! It's my attempt to trigger guilt and shame. It's a surefire way to manipulate and control their behavior.*

Why? Because I know they already feel insecure and powerless. The cold shoulder move simply activates the guilt and shame that are already there. They do the heavy lifting, and I get more power.

DMJ: To summarize, I understand that the egoic-self is your best friend and the energy that sustains you thrives on your Fear of feeling powerless and being made wrong. Essentially it's about your need to be right, agreed with, loved, and in control of everything and everyone. Is that accurate?

ANGER: *Ha! That's only the first layer. Wait until you meet my cousins, Rage and Resentment.*

There is (D)anger in Anger

Perhaps it's no mistake that contained in the word "danger" is another word, "Anger." While our Anger may feel justified, it's always a danger to remain stuck in the energy of Anger. The danger with Anger unmanaged is that it can become an unconscious habit, which is hazardous for everyone involved. Habitual Anger is destructive for the one who is experiencing the emotion of Anger surging through their mind and body, and it can be equally destructive in different ways for those who may be the target of Anger. Anger's descendants, Rage and Resentment, simply add fuel to the fire.

The Good News and the Not-So-Good News About Anger

The Not-So-Good News: *Some of us have been dragging Anger, Rage, and the invisible wound of Resentment around with us for a long time. We've become desensitized to the damage they can do because these toxic emotions have created a home in the infrastructure of our lives without our conscious awareness.*

The Good News: *The emotions of Anger, Rage, and Resentment are all messengers bearing crucial information for us regarding their presence and why they are knocking on our door.*

The Not-So-Good News: *Until we respond proactively, the messenger of Fear, known as Anger and its descendants Rage and Resentment, will continue banging on the door, wreaking havoc and confusion in our relationships and affairs, as well as pain and suffering in our physical body.*

The Good News: *It's never too late to open the door of Self-Awareness and invite these messengers in for a chat. These messengers of Fear are like small children who need something only we can provide—Understanding, Patience, Unconditional Love, Compassion, and Forgiveness. And, they won't cease with their antics until we give them permission to speak. We need to listen and learn, and then let it go.*

28

The Clock is Ticking

For every minute you remain angry,
you give up sixty seconds of peace of mind.

RALPH WALDO EMERSON

As it has been for thousands of years, the world today is fraught with angry people, and most of them do not know that Fear is having its way with them. Have you ever caught yourself angrily reacting to something, flying off the handle unexpectedly? This is a rhetorical question because who hasn't? The real question is, as Emerson infers, did it help or hinder your ability to experience peace of mind and enjoy the gift of your precious life at that moment?

It can be difficult to see Anger as a friend and messenger trying to deliver urgent information when we get caught up in the middle of an "episodic" rant, but that is what it's doing. This messenger of Fear is always on duty, trying to get our attention and enhance our life, even if it requires an angry rant to do so. I use the term "episodic" purposefully because Anger rarely makes a onetime guest appearance. It's the star of a longtime running series that plays on a continual loop through our mind and body.

No One is Born Angry

Adults often get their training to be angry as children when they learn that expressing displeasure through rants, crying and screaming, throwing tantrums, throwing things, and acting scary has a payoff. While no one is born angry, we soon learn the power of Anger. Even if it's unconscious at an early age, it's an attempt at manipulating others. Fear, masquerading as Anger, serves as a motivator to get something. It's a power grab.

Young children are not consciously aware that beneath their Anger is Fear, the Fear of not getting what they want when they want it. And, under that layer of Fear is yet another layer of Fear, the Fear of loss of something. Often, it's the loss of power to control another person's behavior. In this case, it's the loss of power to control the behavior of Mom or Dad. If you have ever seen a child in the grocery store throwing a tantrum because Mom or Dad wouldn't acquiesce to the child's desire for a candy bar or toy, you understand. Most often, the child wins the prize because Mom or Dad can't take the embarrassment or the noise and throws in the towel. SCORE: Child: 1, Mom/Dad: 0. And so on it goes—Anger wins another one. The danger is that too often we drag our Anger into adulthood, where it doesn't belong and is acted out in even more inappropriate, dangerous, and harmful ways.

While the Behavior May Change, the Stimulus Doesn't

*When I was a child, I talked like a child, I thought like a child,
I reasoned like a child. When I became a man, I put the ways
of childhood behind me.*

1 CORINTHIANS 13:11

This insightful quote, attributed to Saint Paul in 1 Corinthians 13:11, is powerful because it speaks to the necessity of emotional maturity and not dragging everything we learned as children into adulthood. As a kid, I carried a lot of Anger. I had a hair-trigger temper that was always ignited by the fuse of Fear, the Fear of being powerless because of my physical size. As I spiritually and emotionally matured, I grasped the dynamics behind this facade of Fear. Anger had become one of my favored practices because, akin to a scared little Chihuahua puppy who fiercely barks at every dog and person bigger than itself, I believed behaving like an aggressive badass would protect me from the bigger kids (and adults). It would be years before I learned to pay attention to that messenger of Fear disguised as Anger, but when I did, it altered the arc of my life. I only wish I had heard and heeded Paul's admonition years earlier.

As we grow older, our Anger morphs into different types of rants and errant behavior, and while the things that trigger

31

our Anger may appear to change, it is stimulated by the same Fear, the Fear of loss of something. It's generally the loss of our ability to control someone's behavior that triggers the Anger.

In extreme cases of Anger, the underlying Fear of loss is often understandable. But, that doesn't make it acceptable. If we have ever been cut off by someone while driving on the freeway and caught ourselves angrily hurling expletives at the other driver, there's a logical explanation for our Anger. We feared the ultimate loss: the loss of our life or that of a loved one. Understandable? Yes! At that moment we were rendered powerless. We lost our ability to control the other driver's behavior (which we really never had in the first place) as he put our life in jeopardy, a legitimate Fear to experience. Acceptable? No! Anger not only endangers more lives, especially if it escalates to road rage, but it's also believed to dump damaging toxins into our body. Perhaps most importantly, it changes nothing that has already transpired.

The Sacred Gap Between Stimulus and Response

Between stimulus and response there is a space.
In that space is our power to choose our response.
In our response lies our growth and our freedom.

VIKTOR E. FRANKL

Let us be clear: When mindfully managed, experiencing and expressing Anger is NOT necessarily a bad thing. The energy of Anger needs to be identified, honored, and ventilated proactively in a healthy way. *How* we deal with that energy matters. As Viktor Frankl reminds us, there is a space, which can be thought of as a sacred gap, between stimulus and response, where a choice has to occur. This is where mindful responsive thinking, rather than reactive knee-jerk thinking, pays off. Mindfulness at that moment helps shape the proper choice we introduce into the gap between stimulus and response. If we don't have the presence of mind to enter that gap and (re)think it through, the messenger of Anger and its descendants, Rage and Resentment, will have their way with us. Giving ourselves a "dress rehearsal" in that gap allows us to witness the potential consequences *before* we act.

If we are consciously and emotionally aware, we can take a deep breath and choose to introduce the practices of Non-Judgement and Forgiveness, both of which can help

33

break the cycle of Anger, Rage, and Resentment. And it all begins in that sacred gap. Easy to say, not so easy to do? Absolutely, which is why they are called practices. Ultimately, with enough practice, we learn that when we cease judging, there will no longer be a need for forgiveness.

Transcending the Messengers of Fear Begins with Mindfulness

If we are mindfully tending to the head and heart in the present moment, the messenger of Fear, disguised as Anger, can actually serve as an advanced scout, very much like an early warning system. To be so present in the moment that we can witness our own thoughts and feelings and then appropriately intercede is the practice of a lifetime. It always begins in the present moment by seeing and feeling the messenger of Fear approaching through the gates of Anger and then recognizing, welcoming, and learning from it. We can't do that if we ignore the messenger.

Mindfulness Practice

Honoring and transcending the messenger of Anger (and its descendants) can only happen in the present moment when we enter the portal of Self-Awareness. The following Mindfulness practice will help open that portal.

- Begin by asking yourself, "How am I breathing?" Take a quick scan of your breath. Is it shallow or deep? Are you mindlessly taking that breath for granted or appreciating the gift it is?

- Realize that very breath tethers you to the present moment, where Life is waiting for you to show up so it may give you remarkable gifts.

- At this moment, the messenger of Fear disguised as Anger is presenting you with a gift. Within the gift is the information you need to transcend the Fear. Do you perceive it as a gift? Realize that until you do, you'll see it as a curse.

- Now, breathe and invite the messenger of Anger to dance with you. You can lead the dance by saying to it, "What do I need to know about you so I may learn how to transcend you?"

If you listen carefully, keeping in mind all that this chapter contains, you'll learn what you need to know. Most often, the answers that are revealed will center on loving yourself and others more and judging yourself and others less.

THE TAKEWAY: Remember, the power Anger seeks exists only when it can terrorize you or others. Make a choice in that sacred gap between stimulus and response to take your power back as you **F**ace **E**verything **A**nd **R**ethink.

AFFIRMATION

"I listen and hold the high watch each day with Emotional Awareness for the approaching messengers of Fear cleverly disguised as Anger, Rage, and Resentment. I welcome them, knowing that through the ensuing conversations I am shown how to transcend them peacefully and joyfully. I celebrate my newfound freedom from Anger, and I am grateful."

Worry

The Second Messenger of Fear

We have approximately 60,000 thoughts in a day.
Unfortunately, ninety-five percent of them are thoughts
we had the day before.

DEEPAK CHOPRA

When was the last time you had a repetitive negative thought? While every thought we have may not be negative, this question ought to make us all stop and consider which messenger(s) of Fear might be running amuck in our minds without our conscious consent. One might ask, "What qualifies as a negative thought?" Any Fear-driven thought we have that restricts the flow of joy, freedom, love, compassion, spontaneity, generosity, and inner peace is a good place to begin. The point is, whether they are positive or negative, the quality, direction, tone, and repetitive nature of our thoughts shape our destiny. So why not become more aware of the thoughts that are stuck on autopilot?

The opening quote by Deepak Chopra is a poignant reminder that there is a need for Mindfulness when it comes to monitoring our thought process and the activity of our many messengers of Fear that pay us a visit regularly. In this chapter the logical question we want to ask is: "If we are repeating ninety-five percent of our thoughts daily, how many of those thoughts are triggered by negative or fearful impulses?"

It requires courage to ponder how often we have repetitive (or compulsive) thoughts that are less than life-affirming. Chopra's data shows Fear has an important message for us if it has been knocking at our door repeatedly in the past twenty-four hours. The odds are, the messenger named Worry is leading the parade.

The Descendants of Worry:
Anxiety & Regret

Do not lose yourself in the past. Do not lose yourself in the
future. Do not get caught in your anger, worries, or fears...
Anxiety, the illness of our time, comes primarily from our
inability to dwell in the present moment.

THICH NHAT HANH

There is a razor-thin line between what was, what is, and
what shall be, because the past and future are imaginary
boundaries in our mind that are perceived and interpreted
in the present. Instead of paying attention to the present
moment, we're usually anxious about the future or regretful
over the past. When driven by Fear, straddling that invisible
boundary leads to Anxiety, which, as Thich Nhat Hanh points
out, is the illness of our time. Between pandemics, political
polarization, a global environmental crisis, and a wobbly
economy, most of us will agree that Anxiety, one of Fear's
most neurotic descendants, has had the run of a lifetime in
recent years.

Anxiety: Compared to its more mild-mannered cousin,
Worry, when Anxiety consumes us, it boosts our adrenaline
output and clouds our thinking mind, which then triggers
uninformed, rash decisions that lead to regretful conse-

quences in the future. In other words, while it is a present-moment experience, Anxiety sucks the life force from us by fearfully ramping up our minds and sky-rocketing us out of our bodies in the present moment and into a nonexistent future. Through the practice of Meditation and Mindfulness, we can recall our Anxiety-driven minds. By breathing deeply and intuiting the otherwise indiscernible line called the present moment, we anchor ourselves there.

The present moment is our only point of power, so we can make a commitment to hanging out there more often by letting go of what no longer serves us and embracing what does. In the process, we will witness Anxiety disappear into the nothingness from which it came...a fearful mind.

The quintessential question each moment invites us to explore is: "What form of Fear might we be clinging to now that is causing Anxiety, and what's more important is, is it serving any useful purpose?" Irrespective of whether it has wrapped its tentacles around the past or the future, Anxiety has no business or power in the present moment when we stay grounded there. As difficult as it may seem, when the messenger of Fear's neurotic cousin, Anxiety, pays us a visit and tries to push us into a future that doesn't yet exist, with Mindfulness we can choose not to lose ourselves in its vortex.

Regret: Regret has the messenger of Worry's back because they share one thing in common: While they may make strange bedfellows, paradoxically, they both want nothing to do with the present moment. Author Eckhart Tolle nailed it when he wrote, "All negativity is caused by an accumulation of psychological time and denial of the present. Unease, anxiety, tension, stress, worry—all forms of Fear—are caused by too much future, and not enough presence. Guilt, regret, resentment...are caused by too much past, and not enough presence." While philosophically they travel in opposite directions on the freeway of life, ironically the messenger of Worry's closest descendant is Regret, a remorseful energy that draws its life force from the past rather than the future.

Regret is always staring in the metaphorical rearview mirror of life, wishing what happened yesterday, last year, or twenty years ago could have happened differently, or better yet, not at all. While Regret masks Fear in a new guise, it is nevertheless Fear's emissary. The Fear that Regret clings to is rooted in the "would have, could have, should have, but didn't" syndrome that only serves to trigger a visit from yet another messenger of Fear, Shame (more about Shame later).

Whether it's an attachment to how something in the future "might or might not" turn out or to the past and how something "should" have been different, the messenger of Worry and its descendants, Anxiety and Regret, are on call every day and only one thought away. The question is: "What can we learn from them that will help make today less stressful and more peaceful, joyful, and meaningful?"

41

Interview with Worry

DMJ: Hello, my old acquaintance. It has been a while since you and I have danced. Looking back at our relationship over the years, I wonder what I ever saw in you. Do you think you can justify what value you are to me or anyone else? What is your message for us, and why don't you just deliver it and then go away and stay away forever?

> **WORRY:** *Stay away? Who, me? My sole goal and purpose in your life is to get as close to you as I can so I may help you control the future (as if that were even possible) and avoid all potential loss. I am not complaining, but that is a twenty-four-seven job for me. Whether it's ten minutes or ten years from now, I just know something horrible could happen, and I am on a mission to help you remember this and avoid that loss at any cost, even if it is at the cost of your peace of mind and well-being.*

DMJ: There they are again, those two pesky words: Control and Loss. The Fear of overall loss, particularly the loss of control, plainly appears to be a major concern for all of you messengers of Fear. Could you tell me why that is?

> **WORRY:** *I am just the messenger, so don't shoot me. We already know that your every Fear concerns the loss of something, so blame that issue on the great granddaddy of*

all my descendants, Fear. What a great self-perpetuating quagmire I create on your behalf. Unless you stop me, I may suck the life force and dreams from your tomorrow. I have been doing that flagrantly and flawlessly forever, it seems. Trying to control the future is what I live for because without it I wouldn't exist.

DMJ: You are a well-known master of projecting visions of doom and gloom into the future. I notice that you conjure the spirits of Dread and Doom often when occupying someone's mind. Isn't that a little dramatic? A bit over-the-top?

WORRY: *Big drama gets big results! Dread, Doom, and Stress join forces with me regularly to help amplify your expectations and experience of Fear. Their aid gratefully enables me to concentrate more on the billions of people who actually think they can evade having a conversation with me merely by consuming anything that muffles my voice.*

DMJ: What do you mean by "consuming anything"? You seem to be quite skilled at keeping people from focusing on the things they are called to do *today* to build a happy, joyous, peaceful, and fulfilling future. Like a magician, distraction appears to be where you draw much of your power. Is it possible that you covertly use the specific distraction known as "instant gratification" because it offers us something to focus on other than you? That is a pretty devious move, you know.

WORRY: *I am all in when it comes to distracting people from their potential for happiness, joy, and especially inner peace. Anything you put into your mind or body to avoid experiencing my presence serves as a wonderful distraction. Instant gratification has worked beautifully as a veiled diversion, a way to keep people stuck in the problem rather than finding the solution. Whether it's food, drugs, alcohol, adrenaline-rush activities, binge-watching television, social-media addiction, gratuitous sex, workaholism, or shopping trips to the mall, I will still be there when you return to the present moment.*

DMJ: I know you are no stranger to the nearly 8 billion people on the planet. What does it take to sustain your popularity with so many people, all of whom are preoccupied with you and what might or might not happen tomorrow?

WORRY: *First, it requires an overactive imagination to do my job. My motto is, "Expect the worst again, and again, and again, ad infinitum." Isn't an obsessive preoccupation with a future that doesn't yet exist wonderful, especially when it affects billions of people so much of the time? Sadly, I have no life of my own, other than in their minds, which gladly results in my omnipresence. I am everywhere, all the time, which means I am always on call...just one worrisome thought away.*

Worry: The Sneaky Burglar

Because it often operates in a quiet, more subdued, and internalized manner, the messenger of Worry doesn't get the press coverage that Anger, Rage, and Resentment do. It's not really news that the three of them disseminate the energy of Fear through our lives in ruinous and aggressive ways. Yet Anger, Rage, and Resentment have nothing on their relative, Worry, which ruins lives just as effectively but more covertly.

Worry is like a sneaky burglar. It stealthily moves through the deepest and darkest corners of our mind and steals the joy and optimism from our tomorrow long before we even get there. The other news is that Worry robs us of our confidence, belief, and faith by holding a dark vision of our future, irrespective of the timeline.

But, there is some potentially good news as well. If we are willing to read between the (head)lines, we'll see that, in an unexpected way, the messenger of Worry has a good side, which is why we don't necessarily want to ignore it. Let us explore both sides of the news about Worry.

The Good News and the Not-So-Good News About Worry

The Not-So-Good News: *The moment human beings discovered their ability to think thoughts that projected them into a* *future that didn't yet exist, Worry, fathered by Fear, gasped its first breath of life, and it has been thriving ever since.*

The Good News: *Likewise, the moment human beings discovered their ability to become self-aware and observe their own minds and emotions at work, the infinite potential for freedom from Worry was born.*

The Not-So-Good News: *The messenger of Worry can disguise itself in many convincing and apparently well-meaning costumes, such as good intentions, care and concern about others, and pious selflessness. A word of caution about these sometimes unconscious hidden agendas is that they can become seductive, self-sabotaging traps.*

The Good News: *By first perceiving Worry with Mindfulness and understanding that it originates in a Fear of loss, it can then be seen as a wise friend, encouraging us to have a passing look at the future rather than obsessing over it. Recognizing that we, alone, can choose how we will experience the future frees us from an incessant cycle of Fear.*

An Affirmation Worth Repeating: "No Worries!"

That the bird of worry flies over your head, this you cannot change, but that it builds a nest in your hair, this you can prevent.

CHINESE PROVERB

Have you ever heard the phrase "No worries" used when someone offers an apology to another or asks that they be pardoned for some small, innocent breach of conduct or etiquette? The term has become a casual but useful euphemism. So if the messenger of Worry is constantly buzzing around inside us all, wouldn't you think that eventually it would wear out its welcome? Beyond heeding its valuable message, if we permit the messenger of Worry to linger too long, the poisonous energy that keeps it alive can taint us. After understanding its message, resolutely proclaiming "No worries" can help us counteract the power of Fear. By consciously using the phrase as an affirmative Mindfulness practice, we introduce a new intention. With Mindfulness, the more often we say "No worries" to other people, the more we will recognize what a great affirmation, or mantra, it is for ourselves. It's another way of declaring that we choose NOT to invest our precious time and energy in something over which we have no control.

We know that worrying makes our mind drift off to a

place beyond the present moment where we have no control. The only thing we actually control is, perhaps, our next breath and the thought attached to it. So why not make that thought a healthy and productive one?

The best way to affect our tomorrow in a positive manner is to be mindfully aware of what we are putting in our mind today. Allowing Fear in any form to take up permanent residency in our mind and body is never the answer to shaping a better tomorrow. I do not mean this to trivialize the issues that may go on in our life or the world, which are intensely compelling and certainly worthy of our concern. It's merely a reality check. Worrying about anything over which we have no control is a poor use of the limited and precious time allotted to us on this planet, because it changes nothing except our blood pressure.

Give the Messenger of Worry
the Litmus Test

There is a time to take counsel of your fears,
and there is a time to never listen to any fear.

GEORGE S. PATTON

The next time the messenger of Worry appears and obsessively wraps itself around us, attempting to cast us into the future, we can stop for a moment and take a deep breath. Then, keeping in mind the acronym for FEAR (**F**ace **E**verything **A**nd **R**ethink), we can ask ourselves: "Is this something we have control over or the ability to change in this moment?" If the guidance we receive is "Yes," then we can thank the messenger of Worry, send it on its way, and take up whatever appropriate action we must to ease the Fear. Conversely, if the answer we hear is a resounding "No," then we can take a deep breath and let the issue go, understanding that clinging to it will only cause more suffering.

Affirming "No worries" can serve as our mantra to be present and relaxed. By being deeply involved in the present moment with high expectations for the future and a low attachment to what that future "should" look like, we can rise above the torment of Worry. When fully embodied, affirming "No worries" can set our minds and hearts free.

Don't Borrow Trouble:
Live in Day-Tight Compartments

Worry is the interest paid by those who borrow trouble.

GEORGE WASHINGTON

When I was a kid, I was what my mom referred to as a "worry-wart." I was consumed with frightful concerns about even the smallest of issues and how they might or might not resolve themselves in the future. As mentioned in a prior chapter, at that time I didn't understand that my worries ultimately sprang from my being small in physical stature. My sense of Shame was crippling, and the Fear of being dominated or bullied loomed large in my mind. Worry became my constant companion on and off the playground. Talk about feeling powerless! That was a heavy burden for an eight-year-old boy. Had I known then that the messenger of Worry was only trying to help protect me, I would have slowed down and had a conversation with it, received the information I needed, and sent it on its way.

My mother, being the wise woman she was, would help ground my rapidly ascending anxieties by saying, "Don't borrow trouble, son. Try to live your life in day-tight compartments." While it took me years to comprehend the power of her loving admonishment, today I get it. By remaining mindful and present in the moment, we can stop what lies in the compartment called "yesterday" (Regret) or "tomorrow" (Anxiety) from seeping into the compartment called "today." Most recovery groups encourage us to live "one day at a time." When we consider the logic of that sentiment, it makes perfect sense.

Today, this holy instant, is all the Creator has given us. It's the mark of great wisdom not to take today or tomorrow for granted, or to squander it on something over which we have little or no control. We can't change yesterday and can't control tomorrow, so, as Ram Dass suggested, "Be here now." I think my mom would have agreed with him. If we resonate with the guidance that allows us to peacefully listen to the wisdom the messenger of Worry brings *today*, rather than ignoring it, we are well on the way to shaping a more peaceful, fulfilling, and joyful life *tomorrow*.

Mindfulness Practice

While 8 billion human beings engage daily with the messenger of Worry, most of us rarely reflect on what this devoted messenger of Fear is actually attempting to accomplish. Consider the following as a Mindfulness practice with the messenger of Worry that will help you honor and transcend it.

- Imagine you are driving your car on an abandoned road in the middle of the night at a high rate of speed, when suddenly a dark figure appears by the side of the road and begins frantically waving at you to stop because of some unseen danger ahead.

- At first your heart races, but as you approach, you realize that the individual flagging you to slow down is the messenger of Worry. Knowing that the messenger has only the best of intentions for your welfare, you slow down and stop.

- Pulling up to the messenger, you boldly roll down your window and query, "What do I need to know about you and the potential hazard ahead so I may get past it?"

- The messenger asserts, "The treacherous intersection of 'What If' and 'Oh No' lies just around the curve. Please slow down and approach it mindfully and carefully because you could lose everything if you are unaware of the hazard."

As you receive and process the necessary information from your messenger, you also access your intuitive guidance from within. You know you can choose to either turn around and seek an alternate route or proceed mindfully with great caution, armed with the information given to you. In either case, you realize your messenger has served its purpose. Smiling at the messenger of Worry, with gratitude for its care and concern, you say "thank you" and wave goodbye.

THE TAKEAWAY: As you vigilantly and faithfully navigate through the darkness, mindfully drawing one breath at a time, you sight a luminous sign up ahead. Examining it, you can discern that it reads: "You Have Successfully Arrived in the Present Moment! Breathe and Be Here Now...Trust and Know All Is Well."

AFFIRMATION

"From this day forward, I choose to perceive the messenger of Worry as a friend and ally. Rather than obsessing about it, I mindfully interact with it by requesting the information I need to understand it so that it won't resurface with the same issue again. I breathe, I listen, I hear, I honor, and I transcend the messenger. Anchoring myself in the present moment allows me to trust and know that Infinite Intelligence always has my back and all is well...all is very well."

Judgement

The Third Messenger of Fear

If you are pained by external things, it is not they that disturb you, but your own judgement about them.

MARCUS AURELIUS

Have you ever struggled to maintain an awareness of the present moment because current conditions didn't "agree" with your expectations or preferences? It's easy for our minds, to be seduced into slicing life into little segmented pieces. The struggle usually originates when we begin slapping labels on everything and everyone, judging what lies before our eyes as preferable or not preferable, right or wrong, good or bad, or less than perfect just the way it is. When we judge, we drive a wedge between ourselves, others, and the wholeness we have come here to experience. The lingering question is: "Why would we intentionally do such a thing and separate ourselves from one another and the wholeness life offers us?"

Just as no one is born angry, it's a fact that no one is born judgmental, hateful, or feeling superior or inferior to anyone else. These are all learned behaviors that come to us at an early age, almost as easily as breathing. Out of all the messengers of Fear, perhaps Judgement is the most difficult to identify because it began lurking in our minds and hearts from the first day we experienced our "otherness" from our mother. Within the first few years of life, we went from a cozy, warm feeling of one-ness to an aberrant sense of two-ness, which was our introduction to a mistaken belief in duality. Suffice it to say, we didn't like that introduction at all. At its best, that realization was disconcerting because it was our first experience of separation from what, until that time, we considered our sole/soul source of nurturing, food, love, and protection. The feeling of oneness from whence we came was Divine.

That was the moment the reality set in (on a subconscious level) that we were on our own, resulting in an unconscious need to protect ourselves by attacking anyone or anything that triggered that sense of "otherness" within us. That is also when Fear, disguised as the messenger of Judgement, knocked on our door for the first—but certainly not the last—time. The operative question is: "What information does the messenger bring us today?"

The Descendants of Judgement:
Superiority, Inferiority, & Hate

The sins of the father are to be laid upon the children.

WILLIAM SHAKESPEARE
The Merchant of Venice

In this ominous quote, Shakespeare implies that individuals, families, cultures, and even countries are all subject to generational visits by the messenger of Judgement. Fear, in its many disguises, is so easily passed down from one generation to the next, without a conscious awareness that it's happening, because it's inculcated in the collective consciousness of the family, culture, or country. Many destructive beliefs are never challenged because of a "that's the way it's always been" mindset. This is when Judgement and its three scions, —Superiority, Inferiority, and Hate—clandestinely enter into our consciousness, worming their way into the crevices and cracks of an unaware mind.

Superiority: Founded in arrogance, the belief in Superiority is driven by the Fear that if others see us for who we mistakenly believe ourselves to be, we will lose our power. The "I'm better than you" syndrome held in place by the messenger of Judgement is driven by the Fear that the opposite actually may be true. Superiority is convinced that, in truth, it is "inadequate," so it performs arrogantly, trying to persuade the world it is sufficient, even to the extent of believing its own act.

Inferiority: While Inferiority appears to be the polar opposite of Superiority, it's not. After all, they are cousins driven by the same messenger of Judgement; only this time it's inverted. Inferiority is Fear turned inward, donning the cloak of Shame. When we judge ourselves (or others) as "less than, or inferior to," we have bought into the Fear of not being enough hook, line, and sinker. Not being enough is an impossibility if we truly believe in our oneness with the Creator of All That Is.

Hate: Founded in ignorance (lack of information) and infused with arrogance (the belief in Superiority), the descendant Hate is an equal opportunity messenger because it believes in both Superiority and Inferiority at the same time. Hate wants to believe it is superior to others, but it fears it is inferior, often seeing in itself what it fears most in others. Hate comes closer to the imaginary divide of "otherness" than most other messengers of Fear. Anyone or anything that challenges Hate's beliefs, prejudices, and intolerances represents a threat to its power and is condemned.

Interview with Judgement

DMJ: Most people would not think of you as being related to Fear, which is, in part, what makes you such a clever and deceitful messenger. Most people aren't even aware that you are making a guest appearance in their mind and heart countless times a day. What is it about human nature that you find it so easy to insinuate yourself into the collective consciousness of humankind in so many subtle ways?

JUDGEMENT: *My job is to persuade you that you are better than whoever or whatever you are looking at or thinking about. It helps reassure you that you are always right, safe, and more powerful. Most humans feel powerless. With self-righteousness comes the sense of power you need to convince yourself that you are in control and safe and that the other's "otherness" isn't a threat.*

DMJ: So, are you saying that self-righteousness is a core operating premise for you? How did you arrive at that conclusion, and why is it so important for us to be right or see ourselves as better than others?

JUDGEMENT: *Obviously, self-righteousness is one of the greatest tools in Fear's vast arsenal. When you weaponize your mind with self-righteous judgement, metaphorically it creates a moat, or an imagined safety barrier, that* *you think separates and protects you from the "other." A perceived duality establishes an invisible boundary line, behind which Fear draws power and creates conflict only as Fear can. Promoting otherness and being perceived as always right keeps me alive.*

DMJ: What I hear you saying is that you thrive on creating a sense of separation between human beings. Is that correct? Is that why your descendants, Inferiority, Superiority, and Hate, are on your team—to help you reenforce and deepen the divide?

JUDGEMENT: *You are a quick study, but first let's clarify that my descendants, Inferiority, Superiority, and Hate, would not even exist if it wasn't for me. They work for me. I created them, and they are at my beck and call. We could say they have to go through me to express their opinions. Also, while they help fortify the team, I would be remiss not to give Ego a shout-out. Ego is like our cheerleader, always there on the sidelines to encourage and cheer us on. Together, we are all on a mission to create and sustain a sense of separation between you and the "other," whoever or whatever that may be in any given moment.*

DMJ: I have heard it said that you rely on great emotionality to enhance your effectiveness. Could you tell me why that is? What power do you draw from our emotions?

JUDGEMENT: *Brilliant observation! Your emotions are like high-octane fuel that drives my descendants and me to perform at an optimal level. Without the power of your emotions, we would go nowhere. Without your emotions fully engaged, we have little power. In order for us to exist, we need your cooperation. We rely upon your unbridled emotions, shortsightedness, intolerance, and inability to practice Discernment and Equanimity. Your inability to stay grounded in an awareness of oneness with life in the present moment is oxygen for me. That keeps the duality of "otherness" in play.*

Judgement: A Survival Skill Gone Rogue

At first, at a primal level, Fear-based judgement functions as a way to survive, but it eventually spins out of control like a runaway train. Being completely immersed in the human condition, especially considering "everyone is doing it," it may seem *normal* to rush to judgement, but it's not *natural*. There is a vast difference between *natural* and *normal*. A rose will never judge another rose in the garden for being more or less beautiful. We don't see the creatures in nature judging one another. They may react to Fear instinctively, and rightly so, but their Fear-based reaction is centered on survival rather than Judgement, Superiority, Inferiority, Hate, or "one-upsmanship."

At the human level, cheered on by Ego and exacerbated by the omnipresence of Fear, our emotions become enmeshed, opening the door for the messenger of Judgement and its descendants to take on lives of their own. While it may not always feel that way, Judgement is a Fear-driven, emotional reaction to feeling threatened by otherness, by anyone or anything we perceive as being separate or different from ourselves.

Because it's so pervasive in our culture, we have become oblivious to the messenger of Judgement when it pops up countless times each day. As our Perspective deepens and our Perception transcends our emotions, we will discover there is some good news and some other news about Judgement, understanding both are prerequisites for our personal evolution.

The Good News and the Not-So-Good News About Judgement

THE NOT-SO-GOOD NEWS: *The messenger of Judgement and its descendants will not be easily evicted from our life because they are deeply ensconced in our minds and hearts. They took occupancy there not long after we slipped into a human skin, and they are very comfortable living there.*

THE GOOD NEWS: *With Mindfulness, we can learn what we need to know from the messenger of Judgement and its* *descendants and then realize we have the power and ability to evict them and send them on their way.*

THE NOT-SO-GOOD NEWS: *When triggered by our emotions, Judgement and its allies arise so spontaneously from within that we often don't even see or feel them coming.*

THE GOOD NEWS: *If we are emotionally and physically aware, we can teach ourselves to distinguish the messenger of Judgement and its siblings as they reach the portals of our minds and hearts. When we are present in the moment, we can mindfully see, feel, and hear them ascend from within, and we can deny them entry.*

Judgement and Discernment Are Not the Same Thing

The ability to observe without evaluating is the highest form of intelligence.

J. KRISHNAMURTI

There's a considerable difference between Judgement and Discernment. Discernment is an observation or perception of "what is" with no opinion or emotion attached to it. If Discernment could speak, it might say, "OK, I see that (fill in the blank), and I have no feelings or opinions about it." We can spiritualize Discernment by opening to and relying upon the input and guidance from an internal Source, Infinite Intelligence, which is incapable of judging anyone or anything because It perceives only the oneness that It is. In either case, Discernment (spiritual or otherwise) transcends the bias of human emotions. Discernment is a filter through which we perceive life nonjudgmentally, with no opinions or emotions attached to it. Discernment and Equanimity complement one another.

Judgement, as we already know, is permeated with a plethora of opinions energized by potent emotions that often cloud the mind and distort clear thinking. If Judgement could speak, it might say, "OK, I see that [fill in the blank]. It's triggering my feelings of otherness, and I feel threatened—I love it or I hate it, I like it or don't like it, etc." Some might question if it's being judgmental when we think or say something positive, kind, and loving to or about another, even with the best of intentions. If emotion is attached to it, it remains a judgement. Even if our words are decorated with lovely lace, ribbons, and bows, they are nonetheless judgmental (sometimes disguised as Superiority or Inferiority) and originate from a place of otherness. It's safe to say Judgement and Equanimity will never be found hanging out together.

Making Assumptions Is Judgement's First Line of Attack

Unlike Discernment, Judgement always draws a line of demarcation between "us and them," rife with assumptions. We make assumptions about other people and situations long before we have actually gathered all the necessary information. To *assume* is to pass judgement without knowing all the details. We make assumptions skewed by our Judgements and then reach a conclusion by building a case to support that Judgement.

Most of us do a great job of applying labels—such as good, bad, right, wrong, preferable, not preferable, wonderful, tragic, beautiful, ugly, fortunate, unfortunate, and so on—on just about everyone and everything. If we stop to look underneath those words and labels and are honest with ourselves, we'll discover powerful emotions and opinions driving them. This is the messenger of Judgement hard at work.

There is Only One of Us Here:
How to Heal the Perceived Divide

We all are born; we all die. We all laugh; we all cry. We all know joy; we all know pain. We all share the same planet, and we all share the same name: Human Being.

DENNIS MERRITT JONES

Could you imagine how it would feel to go through an entire day with no need to seek approval or avoid disapproval and judgment from others? When we peel away the layers of labels we've placed on others and ourselves—looking beyond our Judgements of age, gender, sexual preferences, size, nationality, language, color, intelligence, culture, religion, and social status—we realize we are all very much the same and that it is the labels (our Judgements) that separate us from one another.

We've all come from the same place, our oneness with the Beloved, and it is there that we shall one day return as well. Between those two points is the sojourn we were born to take. Seeing that journey through the eyes of oneness, rather than otherness, is the ultimate resolution to all Judgement. After all, if there's really only One of us here, what's to judge? When we cast the net of Judgement on another person, we also ensnare ourselves. As the great teacher said, "Judge not and you shall not be judged" (Matthew 7:1-3).

Reverence Dissolves All "Otherness"

Practicing Reverence can help us dissolve the imaginary dividing line that Judgement draws between ourselves and the perceived "other." To practice Reverence is to see past the form or illusion of separation and perceive the presence of the Beloved at the center and circumference of everything our eyes gaze upon. If we pay attention and listen closely, the clarion call for Reverence beckons our attention twenty-four-seven. We just need to remember that there is not a spot where God is not.

The Author and spiritual teacher Dr. Ernest Holmes must have heard that call, because it's said that occasionally he dined with a vase of weeds sitting on his table in lieu of flowers. A sacred reminder that Infinite Intelligence flows through *every living thing* equally, and the value (Judgement) we place on a weed versus a rose is the only difference between them.

Living with Reverence isn't all that difficult. It's simply remembering that we exist in a spiritual Universe where everyone and everything is interconnected. Transcending Judgement through the practice of Discernment and Reverence is as easy as perceiving the sacred in a weed. It can be a spiritual experience when we look beyond form and see only the divine Essence therein. It is also true that to perceive the sacred in ourselves is to transcend Judgement and can, likewise, be a spiritual experience.

The practice of Reverence spontaneously initiates a shift in Perception. The filter through which we perceive life is focused and cleansed, and everything we see or do becomes a sacred act. It is then that a direct portal opens in every relationship we have, enabling us to see the face of God. If dining with a vase of weeds doesn't resonate with you, consider gazing in a mirror. Peel away all the layers of Judgement you hold until you can see only the eyes of the Beloved looking back at you. Maintaining a level of Consciousness that goes beyond a sense of duality or otherness can be challenging, but it *is* possible. It begins by seeking a common ground that transcends all otherness.

Listening to and learning what we must from the messenger of Judgement before sending it on its way opens the gate to healing our minds and hearts. The mantra for this chapter is: "Listen, learn, love, transcend, let go, and move on."

Mindfulness Practice

The mystic Sufi poet, Rumi, offers us a wonderful place in Consciousness where we can meet to achieve an awareness of our oneness with each other and life, an exquisite place to transcend Judgement.

Out beyond ideas of wrongdoing and rightdoing, there is a field. I'll meet you there. When the soul lies down in that grass, the world is too full to talk about. Ideas, language, even the phrase "each other" doesn't make any sense.

RUMI

This is Rumi's invitation for us to dissolve all otherness by seeing there's only one of us here. Let us go to that field now.

• Draw a deep cleansing breath as you close your eyes and visualize that your current messenger of Judgement stands next to you. You both talk as you walk on a meandering path that leads to a dry riverbed spanned by a short wooden bridge. As you approach the bridge, you finish receiving whatever message you require to transcend the messenger.

- You spy an open, verdant field populated with wild flowers on the other side of the bridge, wherein everything seems connected and infused with light. The field is a place of pristine peace and beauty, and it silently calls to you.

- Turning mindfully to your messenger of Judgement, you look in its eyes and thank it for sharing its necessary information with you. As you walk slowly across the bridge, leaving the messenger on the path behind, you feel lighter.

- As you stand in the open field, feel the warmth of the sun on your skin and a gentle breeze on your face. All sense of Fear dissolves into the nothingness from which it came.

In this moment, you realize you are free, as the burden of judging anyone or anything—including yourself—is lifted from you. In the presence of oneness, we find only unconditional Love.

THE TAKEAWAY: The meandering path represents our intention to listen to and learn from the messenger of Judgement. The dry riverbed symbolizes our past experiences of duality and a lack of life force flowing freely. The bridge lifts us above and beyond otherness and carries us from the past to the present moment. The field is the fertile soil of Acceptance and Forgiveness, where, with gratitude, we thrive and grow a beautiful life.

AFFIRMATION

"Today, I transcend the need to judge myself or others. I release the past and am open to a future free from Judgement, Superiority, Inferiority, and Hate. Daily, I seek the field of oneness beyond any ideas of right and wrong. Knowing there is only one of us here, I am at peace. I thank my messenger of Judgement for bringing me the exact information when I needed it to heal my sense of otherness. And now I gratefully send it on its way. I am free!"

Selfishness

The Fourth Messenger of Fear

If you wish to travel far and fast, travel light.
Take off all your jealousies, selfishness, and fears.

CESARE PAVESE

C an you recall the first time you felt like you just couldn't get enough of something, so you fearfully held back on sharing it with others? Some might call that mindset "stinginess," some might call it "miserly." But, under any moniker, the messenger of Selfishness was likely present and accounted for.

Most of us likely know what Selfishness is, but rarely do we take time to consider how this Fear-driven behavior impacts our lives and the lives of those we love. Because we are always becoming cause to our own effect, this is vital information to embrace.

We already know that all Fear is attached to a concern of loss of something. Selfishness is driven by a very specific Fear of loss, i.e., losing the power we think we gain by possessing more of whatever represents power to us. Whether it's a child selfishly hoarding his candy from his siblings, someone jealously coveting another person's spouse, or someone being envious of another person's job, status, or income, it's the same Fear of not enough power that drives the action. Selfishness is mired in a belief in the scarcity that there's not enough power in its various forms to go around.

Acts of Selfishness send a message to an unbiased Universe, which operates solely on the law of cause and effect, that we believe in not-enough. If It could speak, the universal Law of Cause and Effect would say, "Yes, if you believe there's not enough to go around, I will help you prove it." The Fear of not enough is a vicious cycle. If we pay attention, the messenger of Selfishness will remind us of how easily this Fear operates just below the surface of our conscious mind, solidifying how "not-enoughness" can overwhelm our senses if we're not mindfully aware of their presence. If we have an honest conversation with this messenger, its input will help us see how blessed we *already* are, which is the first step in breaking the cycle of not-enoughness.

When we cease fixating on what we think we don't have enough of (a practice that only fosters selfishness), the Spirit of Generosity and the Generosity of Spirit will naturally arise from within, lifting us into our original state of Grace and into the abundance of every good thing in our lives.

As Italian author Cesare Pavese suggests, we'll advance faster and farther on our voyage towards a satisfied and affluent life when the Fear-driven messenger of Selfishness is not impeding our progress. At such times, when we may be feeling powerless and uncertain about our "worthiness," the practice is to welcome the messenger of Selfishness onto the dance floor and have a conversation, attentively listening to what it has to say.

The Descendants of Selfishness: Greed, Envy, & Jealousy

The environment that we call society is created by past generations; we accept it, as it helps us to maintain our greed, possessiveness, illusion.

J. KRISHNAMURTI

It's easy to understand why Greed, Envy, and Jealousy are close descendants of Selfishness. They all come from the generational Fear-based belief that someone else holds the good they desire. They want (covet) more of what they believe they don't have, and the only way to get it in one form or another is from "the other." Understanding their motivation will help us locate where in our own hearts and minds they may linger without our conscious awareness. Once we receive and understand the lesson each descendant bears, we can then send them on their way.

Greed: Defined as "a strong desire for more wealth, possessions, and power than a person needs," Greed is an insatiable Fear-driven belief that "more" is better. The question we must ask ourselves is: "How much is enough?" When the messenger of Greed comes knocking at our door, if we can simply pause, take a deep breath, and remember our oneness with an opulent Universe, we can transcend the belief that we need "more" wealth, "more" possessions, or "more" power to live a life of wholeness, purpose, and meaning. "More stuff" is a misnomer for happiness.

Envy & Jealousy: In the bloodline of the descendants of Fear, it could be said that Envy and Jealousy are kissing cousins because they are very close to one another and are sometimes difficult to differentiate. In the context of this book, Envy can be defined as "wishing we had something that another person has," and Jealousy can be defined as "wishing we had someone that another person has in his or her life." The differentiating words between Envy and Jealousy are "something" and "someone." Both Envy and Jealousy are Fear-based emotions driven by a belief in not-enough, which motivates us to covet what others have. Be it a material thing or a human being we wish we had in our lives, the same Universal Principle of Abundance assures us that there's no shortage of either.

In what ways are the messenger of Fear manifesting in our life as Selfishness, Greed, Envy, or Jealousy today...and what can we glean from the dialogue?

Interview with Selfishness

DMJ: I have heard it said that you and your descendants, Greed, Envy, and Jealousy, are the primary cause of much of the world's suffering and poverty, not to mention most of the wars fought from antiquity to modern times. Understanding that you are a direct relative of Fear, what is your motivation?

> **SELFISHNESS:** *Hey, someone has to guard against a short supply of whatever is needed to live a happy life. Why not my descendants and me? We are perfectly trained for the job. After all, "first come, first served" is our mantra and has been since the dawn of time. Nothing has changed but the dates on the calendar.*

DMJ: If I am hearing you correctly, the mindset that sustains you and your descendants is established in a belief in limitation and scarcity, that there's not now, has never been, nor shall ever be enough for everyone. What makes you so certain that your perspective is correct?

> **SELFISHNESS:** *You've heard the saying, "The proof is in the pudding." Just look around. The world is filled with*

want, war, lack, and poverty. It's divided between the "haves" and the "have nots." My long game is to make sure the two never meet. I thrive on separation. The wider the chasm is between me and "the other," the better.

DMJ: Clearly, like many of your descendants, you are dedicated to creating, maintaining, and perpetuating the collective belief in separation between human beings. You accomplish that by amplifying the Fear of not-enough of whatever is required to live abundant, happy, whole lives. You have been pulling the wool over humankind's eyes for tens of thousands of years with the same nonsense, but your ploy appears to be working well. To what do you attribute your longevity and success?

SELFISHNESS: *As a devout messenger of Fear, I know it's human nature to focus on the proverbial glass as half empty. As long as you all maintain that perspective and engage in that form of thinking, I am gold!*

DMJ: You imply that fixating on what we believe we don't have perpetuates the cycle that leads to Selfishness. How is that even possible? How can we fixate on something we don't have?

SELFISHNESS: *Easy enough. That's when I call on my cousins, Envy and Jealousy. Their specialty is looking over their neighbor's fence, lusting for what they see there,* *and thus embellishing their own sense of not-enoughness. Whether it's a material thing, person, job, lifestyle, or social status, it's all fair game for my cousins. They are experts at fixating on what others have and coveting it.*

DMJ: And your descendant, Greed? Isn't Greed just another version of you, but on steroids? You are both so similar; how do you and your cousin even manage to get along?

SELFISHNESS: *We stay out of each other's lane. Greed wants it all and makes no bones about it. My cousin is overtly expressive and insistent, with a "take no prisoners" outlook. I am much more subtle than that. I lie in the proverbial weeds, while subversively doing my work planting seeds of Selfishness everywhere. Along with my descendants, we exist to serve you in making sure you get your "fair share" first, before anyone else does. That's the only way we roll. Our motto is, "All for us and, umm…us for us."*

The Belief in "Not-Enough" Creates an Unseen Chasm

Beware of over-concern for money, position, or glory. Someday
you will meet a man who cares for none of these things. Then
you will know how poor you are.

RUDYARD KIPLING

Until we become the conscious observer of our own mind and witness how it operates, it's easy to miss the subtle motivation that drives the Fear-mongering messenger of Selfishness and its descendants. In their pursuit for more power, these messengers covertly disappear below the radar of our conscious awareness and create an imperceptible gap, not only between ourselves and others, but also between ourselves and an abundant life.

Expanding at the speed of light, perpetually creating more of Itself from within Itself, the Universe offers a plethora of "more than enough." Quantum physicists tell us that the potential for everything *first* exists as unformed energy waiting to be sublimated and given form through our thought and belief system. Ralph Waldo Emerson articulated this principle beautifully when he wrote, "We see the universe as a solid fact. God [the Creative Principle] sees it as liquid law." It's all etheric energy until we give it form. The hook is that we must have the Perception and the Consciousness to see possibilities through the eyes of the Creator, then name it and claim it with an abiding faith. Whether material possessions, relationships, or intangible qualities like time, talent, health, respect, and love, the Principle of Abundance guarantees an unlimited supply.

The Principle of Abundance: The Source of More than Enough

The secret to Life lies directly in front of us every moment of every day. But we fail to see it, perhaps, because like the fish in the water, we are so close to our Source we can't see we are swimming in Abundance. It is the 'nature' of the Universe to bestow upon all sentient forms of life an abundance of whatever is needed, not just to survive, but to thrive.

DENNIS MERRITT JONES
The Art of Abundance

There's no place or time that the Principle of Abundance can be better used than when we are entangled in the illusion of scarcity, the roots from which the weeds of Selfishness, Greed, Envy, and Jealousy spring. Remembering our new acronym for Fear as "**F**ace **E**verything **A**nd **R**ethink," rather than "**F**orget **E**verything **A**nd **R**un," marks the beginning of a remarkable shift in Consciousness. It encourages us to stop, breathe, turn, mindfully look in the eyes of the beast we've been running from, and rethink everything. When we train ourselves to look beyond appearances that at first glance may frighten us, we are leading the dance with the many messengers of Fear. This is especially true of Selfishness, Greed, Envy, and Jealousy. With the awareness of our oneness with Something larger than our Fear, which is the Source of our supply, comes the ability to see life through new eyes. Everywhere we look we'll find the Principle of Abundance flowing freely, operating without refute or restriction.

Closing the Gap Between
Selfishness and Selflessness

To thoroughly access this Principle, we must first recognize and cross the chasm between Fear-driven *Selfishness* and Love-motivated *Selflessness*, understanding there's a *big* difference between the two: One is exclusive, and the other is inclusive. Merging the concepts of "me" and "we" leads to a natural transcendence of Selfishness. As this happens, we awaken to our oneness with a Universe wherein all good, all supply, is abundantly given to anyone who has the mindset (Consciousness) to receive it. And then Selfishness becomes a nonissue. However, there is a price to pay before achieving that mindset.

Evolving from a consciousness of Selfishness to Selflessness is not a move to be taken casually because it's a commitment to living from an entirely different paradigm. Once that commitment is made, we'll realize we have thoroughly entered the flow of an abundant Universe that operates on the Principle of Reciprocity, i.e., that which we give freely and selflessly returns to us in the same manner, with Grace and ease. Likewise, that which we hesitantly or resentfully give with possessiveness and miserliness returns to us in the same manner, with struggle and an abundance of more "not-enough." This is the Law of Attraction impeccably at work. Until we recognize and listen attentively to what they have to say, the messenger of Selfishness and its relatives Greed, Envy, and Jealousy will continue to contribute their energy to the not-enough syndrome. Fortunately, there's good news.

The Good News and the Not-So-Good News About Selfishness

THE NOT-SO-GOOD NEWS: *Selfishness is a way of life for billions of people around the planet because a Fear-based belief in scarcity has been inculcated in the collective consciousness of humankind. Energized by a belief in not-enough, Selfishness is generational. It is modeled and passed down by unaware parents to the open and impressionable minds of their young children, and on and on the cycle seems to go.*

THE GOOD NEWS: *The antithesis of Selfishness and the belief in scarcity is Selflessness, an act demonstrated by an up-close and personal relationship with the Principle of Abundance. Parents inspired by a belief in "more-than-enough" can show and instill Selflessness in future generations. As Selfishness gives way to Selflessness, the world becomes a better place now and tomorrow.*

THE NOT-SO-GOOD NEWS: *Selfishness, Greed, Envy, and Jealousy are pervasive and often difficult to self-detect because they extend into nearly every aspect of one's life. These messengers can also be devious and manipulative, sometimes disguising themselves as their antithesis, Selflessness and Generosity. With their hidden agendas, these Fear-driven messengers have little trouble hiding behind supposed "good intentions."*

THE GOOD NEWS: *An awakened mind knows that it is the intention behind our actions that defines us. Acts of true Selflessness are initiated and guided by an open heart that has no agenda other than to share what good there is with others. Arising from an awareness of our oneness with the Principle of Abundance, the Spirit of Generosity, energized by the Generosity of Spirit, affirms there is always more than enough to go around.*

THE NOT-SO-GOOD NEWS: *The media and Main Street merchandisers work hard to convince us that scarcity is a reality that threatens our way of life. We are bombarded daily with* *the messages that "something" is missing in our life, and that without that "something" we can't be content, whole, and fulfilled. So, we find a way to buy, borrow, or steal it, believing that special "something" will make us whole and complete, which it never can. This Fear-based misconception spawns countless messengers of Fear with Selfishness, Greed, Envy, and Jealousy on the leading edge.*

THE GOOD NEWS: *Without the Fear of not-enough to subsidize their ventures, Selfishness and its descendants quickly deplete their energy by trying to convince people that scarcity is a real thing. A perception of scarcity, however, is not always accurate because it can be an illusion. The messengers of Selfishness, Envy, and Greed will always avoid commingling with the Principle of Abundance because they know they have no power there.*

Balancing the Spirit of Generosity with the Generosity of Spirit

When we liberate ourselves from the grasping tentacles of Selfishness, Greed, Envy, and Jealously, we will experience a noticeable shift in our energy as the Fear of not-enough dissolves. Ascending in Consciousness and merging with the infinite Source of our supply seems to go hand-in-hand as our Perspective and Perception find new ground and clarity.

With a clear Perspective of our oneness with an abundant Universe comes a natural sense of Generosity that flows to, through, and *from* us. This is when our Perception focuses on something as miraculous as when the Generosity of Spirit and the Spirit of Generosity commingle and become one.

The Generosity of Spirit moves through us in a manner that allows us to realize and share the totality of who we are as spiritual beings. Accordingly, this energy then ignites our Spirit of Generosity, allowing us to share what we have and can do as human beings. Finding a balance between the two is the practice of consciously being in the flow of life. It just happens to be the rarified air where the messenger of Selfishness and its descendants Greed, Envy, and Jealously fear to tread.

Mindfulness Practice

Throughout the world, there are basically two types of people: Givers and Takers. This dynamic could be referred to as the WIIFM principle, which is an acronym meaning one of two things: "What's In It For Me?" or "What's In It From Me?" Selfishness and its descendants continually and fearfully live in the question, "What's In It For Me?" because they all want something. Conversely, when we transcend the Fear of not-enough, our Perspective changes and we see the same acronym through new eyes, asking, "What's In It From Me?" How we choose to respond to the WIIFM principle not only defines us—it shapes our destiny.

- As you take a deep breath, close your eyelids and open your Mind's eye. Call forward the messengers of Selfishness, Greed, Envy, and Jealousy…and wait to see which appears.

- This is a call for self-honesty. If no messenger shows up, that is a wonderful thing. It means you have mastered the Fear of scarcity and transcended any attachments to a belief in not-enough in every area of your life.

- If one or more messengers appear, it means they have something to tell you about the Fear of not-enough that lives within you. Are you willing to receive their message and learn from it? If so, listen intently.

- As your messenger speaks, embrace the message and ask, "What's In It For Me?" In this area of my life, why am I so attached to the Fear of swinging across the chasm from Selfishness, Greed, Envy, or Jealousy to Selflessness, to the belief in more-than-enough? What Fear of loss am I experiencing?

- Hold this issue in your mind and know you are one with the flow of an abundant Universe. Then earnestly ask yourself, "What's In It From Me?" How can I enter the flow more fully by extending to others the good I enjoy, not because I should, but because I can? Then watch the Fear vanish as the level of your "I-am-enoughness" skyrockets.

Thank your messenger of Fear, and with a grateful heart watch it return to the nothingness from which it came.

THE TAKEAWAY: The chasm between "For Me" and "From Me" is expansive and deep. Swinging across the chasm from Selfishness to Selflessness reflects the degree of our faith in our oneness with the Source of our abundance in every form, and our ability to flow with It. Consider this Mindfulness practice to traverse the chasm of WIIFM.

AFFIRMATION

"Realizing my unity with a vibrant Universe allows me to listen to the messengers of Selfishness, Greed, Envy, and Jealousy with an open mind and heart, without hesitation. I value their input, and as a result I experience a "more-than-enough" Consciousness in every area of my life. With a grateful heart I celebrate the abundance that is mine to share."

Shame

The Fifth Messenger of Fear

What do you consider the most humane?
To spare someone shame.
What is the seal of liberation?
To no longer be ashamed in front of oneself.

FRIEDRICH NIETZSCHE

Do you ever feel the pain of rejection or the sting of criticism from others? Occasionally, do you look in the mirror and grimace at what you see? Have you ever compared yourself with others and wound up feeling "less" than them? Do you look to others for approval or validation? Have you ever felt disgraced, humiliated, or mortified by something you, or someone else, said or did? Have you ever blamed yourself harshly for making a mistake, and then continued to beat yourself up long after the mistake was made? Do you ever experience the feeling of abandonment by others when they withdraw their physical presence, support, love, and affection from you based on something they infer you did or didn't do?

If we answered "yes" to any of the previous questions, it's likely that the messenger of Shame, or one of its descendants, is stopping by to say "hello." Perhaps we aren't aware of it, but they come bearing a vital and life-changing message.

In the previous chapter, the messenger of Selfishness and its minions Greed, Jealously, and Envy exposed us to the Fear of not "having" enough. In this chapter, the messenger of Shame and its descendants Embarrassment, Guilt, and Perfectionism will enable us to dance with the Fear of not "being" enough.

The Descendants of Shame: Guilt, Embarrassment, & Perfectionism

One of the deceiving things about Shame is that it hides in the darkness between the Fear of "making" a mistake and "being" a mistake. Guilt, Embarrassment, and Perfectionism linger in the shadow of Shame.

DENNIS MERRITT JONES

As we already know, the origin of Guilt, Embarrassment, and Perfectionism arises from a shared common source. They all ascend from Fear and contaminate the moment with more of the same. The Fear of *making* a mistake or the Fear of *being* a mistake are both Shame's favorite activities. What we may not know is that embracing the messages that the descendants Guilt, Embarrassment, and Perfectionism bear requires an unrelenting willingness to look beyond appearances with Optimism, Faith, and the ability to let go of "what was" in favor of "what can be." These three descendants of Shame actually serve us well when we can hold them lightly in our metaphorical dance as we listen to them share what we need to know to transcend them.

GUILT: Many people use Guilt to punish themselves, thinking that somehow it pleases God. This is not only delusional thinking, but it's an impossibility because Infinite Intelligence is incapable of Judgement and thus deriving pleasure from a mistake we've made, let alone punishing us for it. However, we do a more than adequate job of doing just that, punishing ourselves.

When Fear-driven, we may use Guilt as a weapon to punish ourselves or others for mistakes that have been made. But, wait! What if Guilt has a silver lining? What if "some" Guilt can serve us well? Let us be clear that to demonize all Guilt would be like throwing out the baby with the bathwater. With a proactive perspective, some aspects of Guilt can be productive in beneficent ways. As sportscaster Joe Buck said, "I think guilt can be good to a small degree, to keep you on the right path."

When the descendant named Guilt visits us, it can remind us we have an opportunity to up our game, to do the right thing, to *do* and *be* better tomorrow than we were yesterday. Suffice it to say, to *think* the right thing is good, to *say* the right thing is appropriate, but to *do* the right thing is what defines us. When perceived through the eyes of Self-Awareness, Guilt can have a softer side, motivating us to be kinder, more loving to ourselves and others, and less judgmental as well.

Fear becomes the driver when we go on a Guilt trip, using it as a metaphorical hammer to beat up ourselves (or others) for past mistakes, especially when we erroneously believe that somehow we deserve it or that it pleases God. God doesn't linger in the past, nor should we. We have no business dragging the past into the present, especially when we use the events of the past only to perpetuate more Guilt and Fear in our lives in the present moment.

Listening to the messenger of Guilt with a teachable, discerning mind and an open heart is the mark of a wise person. Learn from the messenger and then send it on its way.

EMBARRASSMENT: Embarrassment is one of Shame's go-to emotions because it shape-shifts into whatever is most "inappropriate" in the moment for us and then hangs our Fear right out there, flapping in the breeze for the entire world to see. If Shame was a baseball team, Embarrassment would be the utility man, pinch-hitter, starting pitcher, relief pitcher, shortstop, catcher, manager, and the MVP—not to mention the team mascot! During a tense moment in a game, the manager may make changes to strengthen a weakness on the field out of Fear that the other team may expose it or take advantage of that weakness. In other words, the team is showing their Fear for all to see. Sometimes the changes work. Sometimes they don't. That's when the manager takes the responsibility, which can be embarrassing. It could be said that Embarrassment wears many different hats, under all of which the master messenger Fear lingers in its many disguises.

Embarrassment can be triggered by other people—or worse yet, it can be self-inflicted. Feeling confused, self-conscious, mortified, discomforted, nervous, worried, flustered, distressed, disgraced, humiliated, dismayed, chagrined, and uneasy are just a few symptoms that may arise when the descendant Embarrassment pops in for a guest appearance.

Under any circumstances, whenever the descendant Embarrassment emerges, it is a facade, a stand-in, a front man for Fear. Remembering that all Fear is attached to a concern of loss of something, Embarrassment is attached to a Fear of loss of face, the Fear of being exposed as a fraud, of being less than perfect, which is why Embarrassment and Perfectionism are so closely related. Whether we are feeling embarrassed on our own behalf or on behalf of someone else, we may be assured that our ego is taking a direct hit.

Transcending the Fear of Embarrassment is easy. It's about becoming so comfortable in our own skin that we let go of the need to look perfect in the eyes of the world. Easier said than done, right? Keep reading!

PERFECTIONISM: Perfectionism is the pretty cloak we wear to conceal our Shame. It's one of the primary purveyors of the not-enough syndrome: "I'm not enough, so I need to conceal who I believe myself to be." As we have already established, all Fear is attached to a concern of loss of some sort. In this case, it's driven by the Fear of losing the power that comes when we *temporarily* gain the love, approval, and acceptance of others. Suffice it to say, the messenger of Perfectionism has some serious control issues.

Driven by the need to control other people's opinions of us, Perfectionism fiercely takes on a life of its own as it drains the life force from our relationships, crushes our dreams and sense of spontaneity, and extinguishes our ability to experience Unconditional Love, Joy, and Happiness. The overarching mindset is, "If I can just cover up my flaws, I will be able to fool other people into believing that I am really all right, that I am good enough— flawless in fact. Then, once I have their approval, I'll have more power, so I will put up this façade, which looks very convincing to the world."

Whether it's by constructing a "perfect" looking lifestyle or appearing physically "perfect" in every way, if it's motivated by the need to control other people's opinions of us, the Fear-driven messenger of Perfectionism is on the job.

As we read on, we will invite Shame and its descendants onto the imaginary dance floor and listen with peaked interest to what they have to share. The real question is: "Amid the emotional pain, frustration, and embarrassment, are we willing and able to listen to and receive their messages?" Let us move forward with Confidence as we chat with these particular messengers of Fear.

Interview with Shame

DMJ: As a purveyor of Fear, you and your descendants likely influence more people than many of your messenger peers, and yet a substantial percentage of the human population have no clue who you are or that you are actively stirring up trouble in their lives. Your presence seems so innocuous it almost feels natural. Could you tell me, what is the source of your origin, and what role does Fear play in motivating you to invade so many people's lives without them knowing you are making an appearance?

> **SHAME:** *The source of my origin? You didn't think that the Fear of "not-enough" was limited only to the material aspects of your life, did you? Spreading the fear of not-enough is my only job. I am a specialist at convincing people "they" are not-enough and that regardless of what they do or how much they possess or accomplish, there is still a hole in their soul where something is missing that would otherwise make them happy, whole, and complete.*

DMJ: I have to admit, you played a major role in my life in my formative years, and, *trust me*, that is not a compliment. You made my life miserable. It was over three decades before I learned who you were and that you had become enmeshed in my life. But when I did, my life changed radically. When I finally realized your presence and listened to your guidance instead of pacifying you, I learned how much of my life-energy I had wasted trying to prove my worth to the world—all because I felt flawed, worthless, and less than others. I can see now I had personalized the belief in my "not-enoughness" in a very painful way. But why did it take the first thirty years of my life before you hooked my attention?

> **SHAME:** *Like many of my other descendants, I am gener-ational. I find a home in people's subconscious mind long before they can even walk or talk. Because I am so perva-sive, just about everyone—your parents, your parents' parents, and their parents' parents—all played host to me, unaware. I also stealthily find a place in people's belief systems through the television programs and commercials they watch, including the mind-numbing social media they are hooked on. And let's also give a shout-out to a few of the major religious institutions! Oh, they love using me to control people. We could say, "Fear rocks and shocks the flocks." In addition, because friends and peers are always comparing themselves to one another, I stay very busy.*

DMJ: Once people know you have been subtly lodged in their belief system most of their lives, how can they evict you? What has to shift in a person's consciousness to transcend the mistaken belief that they are fundamentally flawed, that the wholeness they long for is missing, when in truth it's not?

> **SHAME:** *As corny as it may sound, the best way for people to evict me is to love me out of their lives. An authentic sense of Self-Love is my nemesis, my archenemy, because with authentic Self-Love comes an innate sense of wholeness. And with wholeness comes Worthiness, and with Worthiness comes a sense of being "more-than-enough." The reason I have such staying power in people's lives is that from a young age, human beings have been given the message that they are not "love-able" just the way they are, that they have to be or do something different to be loved, cherished, and appreciated. And the amazing part is they keep buying into that same lie hook, line, and sinker every single time. Sadly for me, when they learn to Unconditionally Love themselves, I lose my job.*

DMJ: You are correct, that does sounds corny. To personalize this, what can Unconditionally Loving myself possibly have to do with transcending you, especially since I've always thought I loved myself? Do you imply that I haven't genuinely loved myself? Carl Jung reminded us that, "Shame is a soul-eating emotion." Are you saying that authentic and Unconditional

Self-Love will automatically dissolve the "not-enough" hole in the soul most human beings feel because of you?

SHAME: *Precisely. What you thought of as loving yourself was your egoic-self trying to camouflage your sense of not-enoughness. Instead of the authentic you, you fell in love with the façades you used to convince yourself and others you were more than enough. By mistaking the many façades you held in place for who you really are, you buried yourself in even deeper layers of Shame. This is when and where my first-cousin, Perfectionism, enters the game. Its job is to provide you with plenty of ways to avoid dealing with how flawed you mistakenly believe you are. Now that's a real shame—and, yes, pun intended.*

The Anatomy of Shame

Work on psychological blocks like shame and guilt—they falsely color your reality.

DEEPAK CHOPRA

Many people confuse Shame with Guilt, thinking they are interchangeable terms when, in fact, while they may be considered kissing cousins who are related, they are quite different. It's crucial to our future that we understand the difference because, as Deepak Chopra infers, the messenger of Shame and its descendant Guilt will distort our perception of reality, while Embarrassment and Perfectionism help maintain the illusion. Before we can interpret their messages, we have to understand their points of origin, their intentions, and the language they speak.

Most people will agree that Guilt is a feeling or belief brought on by the Fear that we have regrettably *made* a mistake in the past, be it five minutes, five years, or fifty years ago. Shame is a feeling or belief brought on in the ever-present moment by the Fear that we literally *are* a mistake, that we are invalid and always have been. While the messenger Shame and its descendants Guilt, Embarrassment, and Perfectionism are all Fear-driven emotions, they are clearly on different missions. The one thing Guilt and Embarrassment have in common is that they enjoy having their cousin Perfectionism along for the ride because it helps cover their tracks, temporarily cloaking them and making them less detectable. The good news is that we are wise to their game.

The Good News and the Not-So-Good News About Shame

THE NOT-SO-GOOD NEWS: *Shame stealthily infiltrates our lives through the back door of the subconscious mind, where it camps out long before we know we have the option to select the ideas and convictions we permit or forbid to enter and remain there.*

THE GOOD NEWS: *Emotional Awareness guides us to examine the beliefs that shape our experience and challenge the ones that don't serve us well. With Emotional Awareness, we can deductively track our feelings of "not-enoughness" back to the place of their origin—a belief system that was shaped when we were very young, one that had little or no filtering capabilities. The good news is that now it does. We are in charge.*

THE NOT-SO-GOOD NEWS: *Maslow's Hierarchy of Needs reveals that some of our needs—such as safety, esteem, belonging, and love—are intrinsic and essential for a totally actualized life as we develop. A Shame-based life can begin forming the moment these needs are with-held from us as children, and we unknowingly drag those wounds into adulthood. Frequently, uninformed parents (and other authority figures) exploit these needs to over-power and influence their progeny by deliberately denying or not meeting those needs.*

THE GOOD NEWS: *Do you remember our new acronym for fear: Face Everything And Rethink? With an open, proac-tive mind and an elevated Perspective, the messenger of Shame and its descendants can be seen as harbingers of a bright and fulfilling tomorrow. When we cease running from our messengers or denying their existence, they can then become our teachers, revealing to us what we need to know.*

Remaining teachable is the practice of a lifetime, especially when we listen to the lessons that our messengers bring to us daily.

From "Am I Enough?" to "I Am Enough!"

The danger of living in the "I'm-not-enough" camp too long is that the belief in "I'm not enough" eventually engenders a belief in "There's not enough," and then scarcity takes root in other areas of our lives. How can there ever be enough of anything good in our lives when we believe *we* are not enough and allow Shame to have a seat at the table for more than a casual conversation before we hit the dance floor? Perhaps it's time to **F**ace **E**verything **A**nd **R**ethink.

When we boldly stand toe-to-toe with our messengers and listen to them explain why they are calling on us, we may experience a liberation of the soul we've never known before. Rising above Shame, Guilt, Embarrassment, and Perfectionism does that. It frees us from the entanglements of yet another aspect of the "not-enough" syndrome.

Mindfulness Practice

The ultimate way to transcend Shame, Guilt, and Perfection-ism is to have a high level of involvement in creating the life we want without the attachment to what others think. Perhaps the greatest irony and dichotomy in life is that we live in a "perfectly imperfect" Universe. All things are perfect until we, with our judgmental eye, see them as "less" than perfect.

The messenger of Shame and its descendants have a soli-tary assignment: to convince us that there's a wide chasm in Consciousness between "I'm not enough" and "I'm more than enough." If we will listen to and learn from our messengers, we'll discover how to easily close the gap. But it's up to us to build a bridge that spans that chasm. The infrastructure of that bridge is constructed with Unconditional Self-Love. Think of this Mind-fulness practice as the first step in transcending the chasm.

- As you draw several slow, deep, cleansing breaths, consider the idea that you exist in a Universe that is perfect in every way. While at this moment you may or may not perceive this, try to move with Faith beyond any Judgements of "otherness" or apartness from the Whole. Realize you don't just live in a perfect Universe; it lives in you. You are one with it. As a fish born into water, you are equally one with the Principle of Life. It flows in you, around you, and through you.

- Knowing you are a microcosm of this perfect Macrocosm, feel its Radiance, Light, and Intelligence permeating every cell, muscle, sinew, bone, and organ in your body. Realize NOW no part of you is "less than" or "not good enough" because you are one with infinite abundance. See the inherent perfection you are spilling over into every relationship you share, from intimate to total strangers. Finally, see it enveloping the entire planet.

- With an ever-deepening awareness of your oneness with a perfect Universe, affirm to yourself, "Perfect God, perfect mind, perfect body, perfect life, perfect me." This realization does not rise from the egoic mind but from the Sacred Heart, the place whence flawless Unconditional Love unfolds Itself.

THE TAKEAWAY: You are not a mistake because you are here by Divine appointment, and God makes no mistakes. Everything you say, think, and do from this point forward is blessed by Infinite Intelligence, the Unconditional Love of the Creator with which you are one, the sacred glue which holds the entire Universe in place and makes it so. And so it is.

AFFIRMATION

"As I boldly, attentively, and trustingly listen to the messenger of Shame and its descendants, Guilt, Embarrassment, and Perfectionism, I appreciatively receive the guidance needed to transcend them and I send them on their way. As a result, I thrive in a Universe of Unconditioned Love, knowing that as I exist in It, It exists in me, too."

Loneliness

The Sixth Messenger of Fear

*The eternal quest of the individual
human being is to shatter his loneliness.*

NORMAN COUSINS

The greatest irony and paradox in life happens at both our birth and death. At birth, upon drawing our first breath (our coming), we entered the human condition entirely *alone*. Likewise, at the time of our passing (our going), as we release our final breath, we will exit from the human condition entirely *alone*. It's a solo journey in both directions, and Aloneness points the way. Yet, the irony is that between those two points, the journey is populated with countless relationships.

The paradox is that while there may be loving family and friends surrounding us, welcoming us upon our arrival or bidding us farewell upon our departure, beneath the density and physicality of our body, which exists in a certain time and space, lies the solitary, timeless, and eternal journey of the soul.

The epitome of the paradox is that the soul knows no such thing as Loneliness because it knows no such thing as apartness from the Whole. This is because Loneliness is a five-sensory human condition, not a spiritual one. The soul only knows its oneness with the Wholeness from which it came. Aloneness is its natural state.

As we make the sojourn to and from the mystery of our oneness with Life, the Creator will never leave us, nor can it, because we are one with It. In other words, while the Beloved One may "let" us alone to discover our own chosen way (also known as free will) through the human condition, It has never "left" us alone. It is closer to us *now* than our very breath, and It always has been *and always shall be*. To realize this truth is the sacred gift to be found in the irony and paradox of Aloneness, even as we exist in the density of the human condition.

Being fully immersed in Aloneness opens the portal to our oneness with the Creator, the Source of Unconditional Love, Light, and Life Itself—a place and space where Loneliness can never enter.

SPOILER ALERT: While we are enjoying basking in the presence of Unconditional Love and Light, the messenger of Loneliness often covertly attempts to "butt in." It tries to subtly emerge from the dark cauldron of Fear and occupy space in our life. Its mission is to put a metaphorical spell on us and create an illusion of separation from the Beloved One and the life we have come here to live. It accomplishes this by casting an emotional shadow that wraps itself around us as it defuses the Light and distorts everything in It. If we are not mindful, it's easy to become numb as we are lulled into the emotional vortex that follows the messenger of Loneliness. It is then that its presence becomes our "new normal" and, likewise, our friend and constant companion.

As existentialist philosopher Jean-Paul Sartre wrote: "If you are lonely when you are alone, you are in bad company." Not only is the messenger of Loneliness bad company, it's one of Fear's most dedicated and ferocious emissaries because it believes in, *and actually thrives on*, promoting a feeling of apartness from the Wholeness from which we came and still are one.

The Descendants of Loneliness:
Vulnerability & Pride

*Vulnerability and Pride are both couriers bearing the message
that Fear is making a guest appearance
disguised as Loneliness.*

DENNIS MERRITT JONES

Loneliness has been the topic of many love songs, generally when someone is the unwilling victim of circumstances that have sequestered him or her from the one person who makes them feel whole, happy, and, well, *not* alone. This is when the two descendants of Loneliness, Vulnerability and Pride, gallop to the rescue, supposedly bringing comfort and companionship to the forlorn victim. The problem is that what they bring is not real comfort, and it is certainly not good companionship. In other words, this scenario never ends well in a love song or real life. Once we fully understand these two descendants of Loneliness and what makes them tick, we can revoke any power we may have invested in entertaining them.

Vulnerability: As with all Fear-driven emotions, the Fear of Vulnerability is attached to a concern of the loss or death of something or someone, which can include the loss of our sense of security, be it physical or emotional. When our Fear of loss escalates, it can understandably increase our sense of Vulnerability, which in turn drives us into isolation and often right into the waiting and open arms of Loneliness. As we reactively close the door to our soul, don our armor, and set up a strategy to defend ourselves, Fear celebrates another victory even before the battle has begun. And duality scores another one. The best way to mitigate the Fear of Vulnerability is to embrace the idea of our oneness with the Source of all Life and all Love, knowing in the sacred space of oneness there's nothing to be lost and, therefore, nothing to defend.

Pride: While Pride may be viewed by some as a positive attribute, it is important to examine the intentions that undergird it. If the egoic-self is involved, it also invites many of its other descendants of Fear to join the party. Too often, the Fear-driven emotion of Pride not only creates an imaginary demarcation line that pushes us directly into the camp of Loneliness, it pretends that Loneliness doesn't even exist. When the egoic-self, which thrives on the belief in duality and separation, gets involved, Pride (driven by Fear) takes on a life of its own by setting the stage for a "me versus them" showdown. This, in turn, automatically gives the messenger of Loneliness a seat at the table.

At some time or another, the messenger of Loneliness attempts to pay us all a visit, and we usually dread it because we confuse Loneliness with Aloneness. We've forgotten that Aloneness is a natural state of Being that ought to be welcomed regularly. We were meant to have the experience of Aloneness as part of our ongoing journey, not only at the beginning and end. It's possible we dread the visitation of the messenger of Loneliness because we don't understand that it comes bearing necessary information that applies to our life today. Let us open a dialogue with this messenger and listen carefully to its wisdom as we mindfully discern its message.

Interview with Loneliness

DMJ: Some people connote a visitation from you with a feeling of being wrapped in a shroud, stranded in a long, dark tunnel with no light where they are separated from the world and everyone in it. Fear arises and tells us there is no way out of that dark place. Is that your intention? Is that why you visit so many of us when we feel most isolated, just to amplify our sense of Vulnerability and our Fear of being abandoned, alone, and trapped in what David referred to as the Valley of the Shadow of Death?

> **LONELINESS:** *Very good insight! Even if it's an illusion, creating a sense of separation from life is my forte. My sole job is to convince you that duality and the shadows it casts are real, and that you are apart from, rather than one with, the wholeness of Life. Irrespective of your age or where you may be spiritually, emotionally, or physically, when you buy what I'm selling, it skews your perception of "what is."*

110

DMJ: Many would argue that a prolonged sense of isolation can be devastating to the altitude of our attitude and overall perspective of life. Those are the times when many people may be tempted to subdue you with instant gratification—some form of self-prescribed "avoidance therapy" such as a trip to the medicine or liquor cabinet, the refrigerator, or the shopping mall, or even by engaging in promiscuous or adrenaline-driven activities. *Anything* to avoid you! Is there any rational place we can go to circumvent you?

> **LONELINESS:** *The old saying "You can run but you can't hide" is accurate because like many of my fellow descendants of Fear, I am omnipresent and not a respecter of privacy. I can spill over into every aspect of your life and be there awaiting you with open arms even before you arrive. I just wait for the perfect time when your guard is down and, boom, I'm there! You could be isolated in Antarctica without a soul around or you could be sitting in a baseball stadium surrounded by 30,000 people, and you still wouldn't be able to escape me. That is what a dedicated messenger of Fear I am.*

DMJ: So, if we can't avoid you, can you tell me how we can live a peaceful and meaningful life without having to look over our shoulder, knowing you are only one thought, feeling, or breath away? Please tell me, what is a person to do when you darken their doorstep?

LONELINESS: *Well, while I shouldn't be giving away trade secrets, I will give you a hint: Just remember, I can only exist in the dark corners of your mind as a figment of your overactive imagination. I literally have no power of my own other than the power you give me. As a messenger of Fear, that's my secret sauce. None of us messengers have one iota of power. We rely on your belief in duality, in otherness. We all specialize in creating the illusion of darkness. YOU are our only source of power. Knowing that Light is really all there is, that's a pretty cool trick, am I right? My hint is, don't be fooled into believing, even in your "darkest" moments, that you are ever alone.*

Remembering to Remember
We Are More than a Body

The more accustomed we become to living solely within our human skin, the more we separate ourselves from our spiritual source. The practice of a lifetime is to remember to remember whence we have come.

DENNIS MERRITT JONES

Remembering to remember that we are more than a skin suit, a garment bag of flesh and bones, is paramount to transcending the Fear of Loneliness. After we land in our physical body, in the span of the years between our coming and going, the awareness of our sacred oneness with Life slowly fades into the background and becomes a distant memory, giving rise to the experience (or illusion) of Loneliness. This is when spiritual amnesia sets in. Not only do we forget whence we came, we also forget that Aloneness is a blessed, natural, nurturing, and necessary part of our journey. Many of us learn to abhor Aloneness because, at some level, we misconstrue it for Loneliness, and it frightens us. Perhaps that's because Loneliness reminds us that the veil between life and death (our coming and going) is very thin. Even though we are spiritual beings at our source, having the power of free will ensures that the God of our Being will never force Itself upon us. But, as we know, that doesn't mean God has abandoned us. This is why we need to deepen our understanding of the difference between the Fear of Loneliness and the Love of Aloneness.

The Good News and the Not-So-Good News About Loneliness

THE NOT-SO-GOOD NEWS: *Because the collective consciousness of humankind is steeped in the Fear of Loneliness, it creates a vortex that draws more of the same. The Universal Law of Attraction never sleeps—like attracts like.*

THE GOOD NEWS: *Loneliness, in itself, is not necessarily a bad thing if we don't lose ourselves in the darkness of its vortex.*

If we can remain conscious and mindfully aware when Loneliness sets in, we can use it for our growth and healing.

THE NOT-SO-GOOD NEWS: *Our tendency is to avoid the messenger of Loneliness by ignoring it or numbing ourselves to its presence rather than allowing it to reveal itself as our teacher. When we do this, Loneliness wins. What we resist persists.*

THE GOOD NEWS: *We can use the messenger of Loneliness as a bridge to something much more rewarding if we are mentally and emotionally present when it visits us. However, we must intentionally lean into it and dance with it instead of being unconsciously absorbed by it. This is when the acronym **F**ace **E**verything **A**nd **R**ethink takes on a deeper meaning.*

Learn to Listen to the Silence

*Welcome the Silence; it beckons you to
come closer to who you really are.*

DENNIS MERRITT JONES

We know that Loneliness creates an emotional void, a sense that we are isolated and separate from the whole of Life. It can manifest as a Fear-driven, soul-crushing, deafening noise (negative self-talk) in our mind that ascends from the egoic-self and dominates every area of our life. Aloneness, however, is standing in that very same void but with an entirely different perspective, knowing that while it might appear we are "alone," we are not lonely because we know in truth we are never alone. Even in our darkest of times, there is a Light burning within us.

It is in our sacred moments of Conscious Aloneness when we are able to intentionally and mindfully turn inward that we are most directly connected to that Light. The practice is to remember the Light of Infinite Presence is there *now* and always has been, regardless of where we may be physically, mentally, emotionally, and spiritually. In the words of Sufi mystic Hafiz, "I wish I could show you, when you are lonely or in darkness, the astonishing light of your being." We were born as Beings of Light, and nothing has changed. We are still one with the Light.

"Be still and know" is more than a spiritual admonition. It is Wisdom ascending from the awareness of our oneness with Something greater than ourselves. Taking time daily to sit alone in Silence is the master's way to transcend the Fear of Loneliness and access an inner Peace that passes all human understanding...one breath at a time.

There is Life After Loneliness

Willing to experience aloneness, discover connection everywhere;
Turning to face my fear, I meet the warrior who lives within;
Opening to my loss, I am given unimaginable gifts;
Surrendering into emptiness
I find fullness without end.

JENNIFER WELWOOD

It is true that as part of living in a human skin, Loneliness will attempt to visit all of us from time to time. Wisdom would dictate that we prepare for the visit with a proactive mind. The next time it pays us a visit, rather than denying it, pushing against it, or struggling to turn it away, we can confidently welcome it with open arms. As we deepen our understanding of the messenger of Loneliness, we can fearlessly embrace it, dance with it, *listen to it*, learn from it...and *then* send it on its way.

If we are willing to mindfully allow the messenger of Loneliness to be our guide, we can follow the tunnel it bores into that place within us that allows our soul room to grow outward. This is the transitional bridge between Loneliness and Aloneness, and it begins with an eighteen-inch journey from the head to the heart. It's a call to practice Equanimity, balancing our mind with our emotions. Learning to embrace the sanctity of Aloneness is akin to taking the first step out of that tunnel of darkness and into the Light of a new day…and perhaps a new life.

A journey of this magnitude may feel too overwhelming to go it alone. If so, there are qualified professionals (therapists, psychologists, and ministers) who can help point us in the right direction. There's absolutely no shame in asking for guidance when we know we are lost in the fog and Fear of Loneliness. The practice is to keep moving forward, trusting that even in our darkest moments of Loneliness, there is a Light at the end of the tunnel.

When we confidently find Peace in our Aloneness, something quite extraordinary happens—like moths drawn unto a flame, the Light we radiate effortlessly attracts the appropriate people and circumstances to us. In the process, we'll notice Loneliness fading into the nothingness from which it came. Always remember that Light and darkness cannot exist in the same space. To the degree we step into the Light, we will naturally move out of the darkness; that is when we'll see there really is Life after Loneliness…and that's a beautiful thing!

Mindfulness Practice

When we sit alone in quiet contemplation of our oneness with Infinite Presence, we will take the first step in accessing our innate and sacred Wholeness, a Wholeness that supersedes all conditions of the five-sensory world. Then, when the messenger of Loneliness comes knocking at the door, we can more easily allow it to enter and listen to what it has to say before proactively sending it on its way. To sit at the feet of this particular teacher and receive its message requires Teachability, Courage, and Faith. Because we know we are one with Something larger than the Fear that Loneliness represents, at the conclusion of the conversation we can welcome the pristine experience of Aloneness that awaits us on the other side of Loneliness...as It always has. Consider this Mindfulness practice as the entry point to a Peace that passes all understanding.

- Have an unlit candle with you as you enter and sit in the darkness of a safe environment. For several minutes, simply sit quietly and breathe mindfully, allowing yourself to feel immersed in the darkness. Breathe deeply and gently settle into your chair.

- Mindfully light the candle and witness the flame casting a gentle glow that naturally dispels the darkness, filling the room with a soft light. Observe the light for several minutes as you continue to focus on your breath. Thinking of the room as the interior of your Being, experience the light that so softly illuminates the room, swirling around you and ultimately wrapping you in its radiance.

- Imagine breathing the Light into your interior when suddenly you realize it's *already* there, that the Light's point of origination is within *you*. The candle is but a beautiful outer reflection of that inner Light.

- Visualize and feel that Light flowing through you, flooding your interior with the Unconditional Love of the Beloved, which goes beyond anything you've ever known. As you internalize the Light, feel It permeating the essence of your Being and saturating every cell, organ, bone, sinew, and particle of your body.

- Finally, bless the darkness and the Loneliness it represents, and let it go. Surrender it unto the Light. Whether your Loneliness and sense of isolation results from Anger, Resentment, Worry, Judgement, Jealousy, Selfishness, Sadness, Shame, or any of Fear's other many descendants, witness it dissolve into the Light.

- As you gently extinguish the flame from the candle, realize the Light of the Beloved still exists *within* you and always will. Embrace the fact that you have done nothing more than remember the radiant presence of the Beloved in that sacred moment and allowed it to envelop your entire Being.

THE TAKEAWAY: It's important to realize that you didn't have to chase the Loneliness away, struggle with it, bargain with it, curse it, or fear it. You simply called forward the Light, and in the process, the messenger of Loneliness faded into the nothingness from whence it came.

AFFIRMATION

"If today, or any day, the messenger of Loneliness pays me a visit, I commit to standing toe-to-toe with it rather than running from it, denying it, or allowing it to lead the dance. I lean into it and listen mindfully to what it has to share with me. Remembering that Loneliness has only the power I give it, I reclaim my power and send it on its way. I do so by moving toward the inner Light of my Being. I embrace my cherished Aloneness, knowing in truth I am never alone."

Uncertainty

The Seventh Messenger of Fear

We sail within a vast sphere, ever drifting
in uncertainty, driven from end to end.

BLAISE PASCAL

Do you enjoy NOT knowing where you are going? Most of us don't unless we are eight years old. That's because the older we get, the more Fear controls our perception of the Unknown. I recall as a kid when my Dad would pile the entire family into our brand new 1958 Oldsmobile 88 convertible on a Sunday afternoon for a "mystery drive." Whether he was taking us to Disneyland, the Dairy Queen, or the beach, he wouldn't tell us where we were going until we arrived at the destination and saw it with our own eyes.

Dad loved keeping us in the mystery of the moment as much as we four kids did. While it drove us delightfully bonkers with anticipation, those mystery trips became the highlight of our weekends. We knew Dad was a trustworthy guide, so the mystery of not knowing where we were going fell into the category of "having fun," and it rocked knowing that at the conclusion of the adventure, all would end well... and it always did. Then, I grew up. The fairy tale was over and the story changed.

With the responsibilities that came with adulthood, the childhood enchantment of not knowing where I was going became a different kind of mystery trip. The older I grew, the more attachment I had to knowing how the story would end each day. It was only then that I realized I wasn't alone on this mystery trip. It became obvious that consternation over an unknown future was endemic in our culture. People everywhere seemed to be consumed with anxiety over an unknown tomorrow.

The misuse of, and addiction to, mind-altering substances (legal or otherwise) in our culture is an indictment of how widespread the Fear of Uncertainty is. While we each may choose to deal with it differently, it affects us all until we grow to understand how to consciously navigate through it. I say "through it" because it's quite impossible to circumvent Uncertainty if we want to move onward, creating a life worth living.

Our attachment to the need to know and control the Unknowable is generally accompanied by a considerable amount of anxiety and emotional suffering. Kahlil Gibran echoed these sentiments when he wrote, "Our anxiety does not come from [just] thinking about the future but from wanting to control it." There are few things more troublesome than a mind that errantly, fearfully, and habitually wanders into the future looking for potential pitfalls and problems and then drags them back into the present moment to be actualized and agonized over.

Normally, this is when one of Fear's most committed and nebulous emissaries, the messenger of Uncertainty, enters the story. This messenger is a trained, combat-hardened specialist whose mission is to embellish our Fears by undermining our confidence in a bright future and the choices we make to get there. Casting shadows of doubt, infused with malaise and confusion that cloud our mind, is this messenger's passion. Its goal is to do anything in its power to keep us from moving onward toward a life worth living. Even in the minutiae of our daily activities, the messenger of Uncertainty seeks to skew our thinking and the choices we make, not to mention our general attitude regarding the future.

The Descendants of Uncertainty:
Change, Doubt, & Procrastination

*Resistance to Change is fathered by Doubt while
Procrastination applies the glue that keeps us stuck. When
combined, they enhance and glorify the Fear of Uncertainty.*

DENNIS MERRITT JONES

Change: The Fear of Change is legion. The only people who look forward to change are babies with wet diapers. Most of us are driven to accept Change by either inspiration or desperation. Too few of us are actually inspired to jump into the Uncertainty that Change brings because it can be frightening. Most of us move forward into the field of Uncertainty because we're motivated by desperation. Desperation is when it hurts too much to remain where we are, where our Fear of staying stuck in "the box of sameness" eclipses our Fear of Uncertainty.

Doubt: There is a wide chasm between Doubt and Discernment. Some Doubt is good if it is first run through the filter of Discernment, separating Fear from Wisdom. Left unchecked and given full rein, the descendant of Uncertainty known as Doubt fearfully lurks in the dark shadows of indecision today in a manner that may affect our lives tomorrow. Doubt leads to a hesitancy to commit to any form of action that could possibly end in a future loss. It's a subtle energy that occupies space in the foreground of a fearful mind because it is looking for what's *wrong* rather than what's *right*. Knowing that all Fear is attached to a concern of loss, Doubt manifests as a loss of faith in our ability to be discerning from our innate Wisdom and Intuition.

Procrastination: This descendant of Fear won't even consider taking any action today that will proactively place us in the field of Uncertainty because its head is deeply buried in the sand of denial, fearfully trying to avoid any action, at any cost. We are often immobilized by Fear when we Procrastinate due to present distractions. Procrastination thrives on instant gratification by kicking the can down the road called tomorrow, fantasizing that conditions will be more favorable then. Dream on.

While their focus is on tomorrow, these three dedicated descendants of Fear can all be very effective at undermining a life worth living today. Fortunately for us, we are one with a Power and Presence NOW that is greater than anything Change, Doubt, and Procrastination can muster. With faith-initiated action, we can learn how to access and trust that Power.

As we conclude our series of interviews with Fear's main minions, we can be assured that this messenger is eager to cast its magical spell of illusion and delusion. It delights in trying to drag us into the dark shadows of our own mind where our feelings run amuck and the decisions about *tomorrow* are made *today*. The difference is *now* we can lead the dance because we are prepared to courageously lean into, listen to, and learn from the messenger. It's time to **F**ace **E**verything **A**nd **R**ethink the mystery of Uncertainty.

Interview with Uncertainty

DMJ: Earlier, we talked with your cousin, the messenger of Worry. We learned that it, too, likes to throttle our minds into overdrive, casting us into an unknown future filled with fearful "what-ifs." How are you so different from Worry that you would deserve your own chapter in this book?

> **UNCERTAINTY:** *While Worry and I both live on the same floor in the commodious home that Fear built, we keep different hours. Worry is obsessively preoccupied with the specific "what-ifs" and trauma-dramas of your future, but my focus is more about the overarching Uncertainty of life itself. It's ALL a mystery, and I will not let you forget that. Albeit more subtle and less invasive, I spread a much wider swath of Fear than Worry by influencing the multitude of choices you make each day that affect every aspect of your life. Consider that! Now try going one hour without making a choice. You can't do it, can you? From*

the massive once-in-a-lifetime choices to the trivial details of daily life, the things that Worry would not even consider an issue, I do, and I will always have your back. Like it or not, I'm there!

DMJ: Are you saying that while you are not as neurotic as Worry, who always seems busy obsessing about the future, you are more covertly widespread and invasive? If so, can you give us an example of how you operate differently than your cousin, Worry?

UNCERTAINTY: *While you may not "worry" about the meal you are going to order as you walk into a restaurant, I am there with you: Will you choose a salad or hamburger or both, and what about that tempting dessert? When you walk into the auto dealership to buy your next car, will it be an SUV or sedan, and will it be electric or gas-powered? Yes, I am with you. When you ponder whether or not you should go to college, I am with you. When you choose to take that new job offer or not, I am with you. Choices, choices, choices…what are you gonna do? Each one you make has consequences. While my cuz, Worry, may or may not help influence these choices, I am always there with you, twenty-four-seven.*

DMJ: So, what I hear you saying is that while you may not always bring your cousin Worry along for the ride, you are a master at casting a subtle but omnipresent shadow of doubt and confusion for our future. Irrespective of the decisions that guide the choices we make—from the small, innocuous ones to the large, once-in-a-lifetime decisions—your presence is there. Is that a fair assessment?

> **UNCERTAINTY:** *Oh, you are good. But, seriously, are you sure about what you just said? Really? OMG! Wait for it…BOOM! Got ya thinking about it again, am I right? That's how sneaky I can be. I enjoy getting into people's heads when they say or do something, clouding their minds with innuendo after the fact. When I can make you second-guess the things you've done or said or plan on doing or saying, I am on a roll. But I can't take all the credit, because one of Fear's greatest champions of innuendo and assumptions, Doubt, has just joined the party.*

DMJ: I'll have to give you that one. When Doubt pays us a visit, it genuinely messes with our minds. Indecision creates a major kerfuffle for most people. When we start second-guessing ourselves, it's a good indicator that you and your cousin, Doubt, have weaseled your way into our minds, sequestering us from our own self-confidence. But there's a remedy for that. My mom, my first spiritual teacher, used to say: "Learn to always doubt your doubts, son." How's that for a double-edged turn-around, giving you a taste of your own medicine? Using Doubt to challenge what we are doubting is pretty clever. While it may be considered a pithy statement, it is powerful. When we begin to mindfully "doubt our doubts," we are on the way to transcending the Fear of you, right? You'll have to pardon me here, but I think it's my turn to say, "BOOM!" Or as my mom would say, "Put that in your pot and stir it!"

UNCERTAINTY: *Whoop-de-do! Score one for you! However, I have more than one arrow in my quiver. You've neglected to mention my other two secret weapons, Change and Procrastination. They are both highly skilled at wreaking havoc and playing tug-of-war with your emotions, particularly your decision-making abilities. The Fear of Change seldom gets the credit it's due. And, Procrastination, well, we'll talk about that one later. Any way you slice it, we all draw our next breath from you and your willingness to be so very open to our input. However, while Uncertainty is my name and malaise and confusion is my game, I can be your friend as well. The irony is that with the right perspective, I can be used as a force for good in your life by helping you create a future worth living in.*

Creativity Requires Uncertainty

The quest for certainty blocks the search for meaning.
Uncertainty is the very condition to impel man
to unfold his powers.

ERICH FROMM

There is a bright side to Uncertainty. As psychologist and humanistic philosopher Erich Fromm inferred, an overdose of certainty stifles our deeper quest for creating a life of purpose, power, and meaning. Uncertainty is the life-laboratory where new creation happens despite Fear's presence. Everything that is imbued with life force is "hard-wired" to push out, to grow and evolve. In metaphysics, this dynamic might be referred to as the Divine Creative Urge.

By virtue of the Universal Principle of Expansion, this Creative Urge is the energy of Infinite Intelligence in action, and It permeates every living thing. In the way it operates, the Creative Urge is declaring, "I must become more tomorrow than I was yesterday." The downside of resisting the innate urge to grow can be summarized by the Universal imperative: "Grow or die." In brief, living things that don't grow die. It's a Universal Truth to say growth is a sign of Life and, therefore, our continued growth is a signal to the Universe that we know our mission here is not finished yet. It's the awareness that there's always more to do. So, we ought to get to it.

The reality check comes when we embrace the fact that there's no such thing as growth in the center of the small, confining box of certainty. We were born to be creators. To accomplish this Divine assignment, we have to be willing and able to come to the edge and step out of the box of certainty and into the open fertile Field of Uncertainty, where all possibilities await our discovery.

We must transcend the boundaries of the known and lean over. Only then can we move forward, venturing beyond our pre-established beliefs and into the Unknown—ready to courageously explore that which is yet to be, the place where all new creation takes place. Easy to do? Of course not. But that is both the *good news* and the *not-so-good news*.

The Good News and the Not-So-Good News About Uncertainty

THE NOT-SO-GOOD NEWS: *We cannot create anything new if we stay within the confines of what we already know. From that stagnant place of certainty, anything new we attempt to create will be contaminated with yet another version of the known…and on it goes. The Universe will allow us to exist in a state of regenerative stagnation for only so long before we're called home. "Grow or die" is Its motto.*

THE GOOD NEWS: *Uncertainty plays a major role in creating an enriched, more meaningful experience of Life once we can transcend our Fear of it. It's a simple case of cause and effect. There must be an induction of new and fresh ideas if we wish to manifest new life experiences. Over 2000 years ago, the apostle Paul urged us to remember this same wisdom in Romans 12:2, "Be transformed by the renewing of your mind." Its validity remains unchanged to this day. "What you sow in your heart, ye shall reap…As within, so without" are words we can "live" with.*

THE NOT-SO-GOOD NEWS: *The Fear of Uncertainty is a powerful deterrent to moving forward because transcending it requires us to pull ourselves up and out of the rut of the comfort zone and go where we have never gone before. However, climbing out of the comfortable rut of certainty is just the beginning. As we leave the known behind and move into the territory of the Unknown, anything can happen. And that's the point! Stepping into the open fertile Field of the Unknown, where all new creation takes place, can be perceived as risky because anything can happen. However, it's a prerequisite for creating a new life—a life we've never known before.*

THE GOOD NEWS: *When we remember our oneness with the Infinite Intelligence that placed us here, we know we are guided, guarded, and protected as we venture into the "Zone of the Unknown." Rather than being dragged into Uncertainty* *kicking and screaming, we go willingly with ebullience and faith, knowing that we go there not alone, and all is well. This is the inherent Wisdom that guides us on the quest. Listening to that Wisdom and acting on it is the mark of one who has transcended the Fear of Uncertainty.*

Transcending the Fear of Uncertainty

The biggest obstacle between ourselves and the greatness we have come here to demonstrate lies in our own belief system.

DENNIS MERRITT JONES

As we have already established, a minuscule number of people will ever say they thrive on not knowing what tomorrow will bring. The question is, are those of us not living in that camp actually thriving? Or are we merely existing as we maneuver to avoid the Fear of Uncertainty? There's a perceived safety and comfort when ensconced in the middle of a metaphorical cocoon of certainty. Albeit an illusion portraying the perfect life, an overabundance of certainty can really be a metaphorical death trap.

While it may appear to be a lot easier to enjoy Life's journey when we are certain everything is going to end well, it's a dead end. If we are not mindful, our Fear of Uncertainty will bury us in the middle of the box of certainty. As the Fear of Uncertainty subtly burrows more deeply into the reticent shadows of our own consciousness, it can paralyze us emotionally and undermine any forward progress. This condition has been described by some as feeling stuck in the muck, yuck, and mire with no path out. This is the place where the part of us that is hardwired to grow goes to die, where we have settled into the complacency of too much certainty.

We know we were given the gift of life by the Beloved to create and that if we don't do so, we dishonor the Giver of the gift. The biggest question is, equipped with this information, what shall we choose to create?

The greatest drawback to being stuck in the muck, yuck, and mire is that if we remain there too long, it becomes the norm. Because we are always becoming cause to our own effect, if we become bogged down in the muck, yuck, and mire, the only thing we will create is more of the same. It's time to break free.

Everything great that has ever been done was, at some point, considered impossible until someone did it. That's because the "someone who did it" believed they could do it by either circumnavigating the muck, yuck, and mire or plowing right through it. Thus the saying, "All things are possible to those who believe." We can each be those people, but it will first require making peace with the messenger of Uncertainty. By listening to what it has to teach us, we can transform this messenger from being a feared enemy into a trusted friend and ally who encourages us onward.

Mindfulness Practice

As a species we are obsessed with (actually addicted to) trying to manage, manipulate, and control the one thing that doesn't yet exist: the future. The question is, how is that working out? For most of us, the answer is generally "not so well." Trying to control what doesn't yet exist not only goes against our natural state of Being, but it's also a fiasco that is impossible to accomplish. Consider this Mindfulness practice as a method of free-falling naturally into the open arms of Uncertainty with a Faith that passes all human understanding.

- Find a quiet place to sit outdoors, preferably in or near a garden where Nature's presence can be strongly felt. If it's not possible to be outdoors, sit by a window with a similar view.

- After breathing mindfully and deeply for several minutes, imagine yourself becoming fully "rooted" in the garden. Focus your attention on a flower, plant, or tree and maintain your gaze until you can sense your oneness with it. Then realize you share the same life force—the same sun, the same oxygen, and the same soil.

- As you close your eyes and open your mind and heart, invite that living thing to be your teacher. Ask if it has ever felt any Fear of Uncertainty, or if it has ever resisted any Change, embraced any Doubt, or considered

Procrastination to avoid being fully present in the mystery twenty-four-seven with all the challenges it may bring. Of course, the answer will be "no." Why? Because it intrinsically knows it is sustained by an Infinite Power and Presence that knows no such thing as Uncertainty.

THE TAKEAWAY: The Universe knows nothing about Uncertainty. Uncertainty is a concept humankind invented to stifle its own evolution and growth because it finds great comfort in "the zone of the known." The takeaway is that if a tree or flower can transcend the Fear of something that doesn't even exist, so can we. This is deep Wisdom we can apply the next time the messenger of Uncertainty stops by for a chat. The practice is to remember it exists only in our mind.

AFFIRMATION

"As I align myself with Infinite Presence, I am naturally lifted above the plane of duality where there is no time and space, no here and there, only the present moment where Fear of loss cannot exist. I transcend the Fear of Uncertainty by locating and living from that place in my mind and heart, wherein the Divine Creative Urge continually nudges me and I heed Its call knowing that all is well on my mystery trip…all is well."

PART THREE

• • • • • • •

Listening to Fear

Facing Everything and Rethinking

*Most dictionaries define fear as uncomfortable, tense feelings
triggered by danger, real or imagined. But more precisely,
fear indicates confusion, ignorance, and a lack of
awareness or understanding.*

MICHAEL BENNER
Fearless Intelligence

Has your Perspective, Awareness, and Understanding of Fear changed since you picked up this book? If it hasn't, perhaps this final section will be of value to you.

If your Perspective, Awareness, and Understanding of Fear has deepened, you can think of this final section as a personal victory lap. It will reinforce and confirm what you have garnered, as well as offer you some added insights regarding the relationship between Fear and its opposite.

As we circle back around and touch base with some key points presented in *When Fear Speaks...Listen*, I invite you to slip into the Consciousness of the Silent Witness. Give yourself permission to perceive this information with Discernment, Equanimity, Openness, and Inquisitiveness, as if you are being exposed to it for the first time. Become "aware that you are aware."

Self-Awareness is an extraordinary gift from the Creator that few of us actually take time to consider. Humankind is the sole/soul recipient of the gift of Self-Awareness. No other living creature has the ability to witness its own mind at work. The ability to think a thought or have a feeling, step outside of our mind and body, and impartially observe (or analyze) that thought or feeling lays the groundwork for a new life. It allows us to engage Life at a more intentional level and play a conscious role in shaping (choosing) our own destiny. It is then that we can use the powerful gift of Discernment to either "embrace or challenge" the thoughts, beliefs, and ideas that pass so freely through our minds and hearts without a "second thought."

The messengers of Fear are all trying to avoid the spiritual speed trap of Discernment. They know they have no power in an impartial, Self-Aware, and spiritually grounded mind. By no coincidence, it is also the first step to learning how to dance with our messengers of Fear. Witness yourself as you read this chapter. Mindfully observe your thoughts and especially your emotions as they arise. They will point out exactly which messengers of Fear are trying to communicate with you now. What you choose to do with that information will play a crucial role in manifesting the life you have come here to experience.

140

The Sojourn to Fear and Back

Life is a stranger's sojourn, a night at an inn.

MARCUS AURELIUS

We will soon conclude our sojourn into the deep and mysterious cavern of our own Consciousness, where Fear and its many messengers have lived rent-free for our entire lives. Now it's time to pause, take a deep breath, and smile. We have come a long way together…but we can't stop here.

The reason I use the term "sojourn" is because, as Marcus Aurelius infers, it marks a temporary stay or stopover some-where—a place we are not destined to remain. The promise of the sojourn lies in knowing we need not linger with our messengers of Fear any longer than necessary to listen to and learn from them. We may consider the Wisdom we assimilate from them as the Light that will help us see and shape our life differently in the future.

Knowing what we now know, we can lovingly put our messengers of Fear on notice that we are aware of their presence. They have gained our attention, and that's a good thing. It's also a good thing to remember our Fears are nothing more (or less) than emotionally-driven thought impulses coursing through our mind and body that have absolutely no power other than the power we give them. The inescapable reality is that over the course of our life, we will have many encounters with Fear in one form or another. Like it or not, it's the price we pay for the privilege of being alive.

The good news is we know this doesn't mean that Fear has to be our constant companion. The reality of this sojourn becomes more obvious as we discover our own true Self-Worth and oneness with God, also known as the Beloved, Infinite Intelligence, Divine Presence, or in this case we may know It as Light. By remembering that Light always dispels darkness, our encounters with Fear can be more brief, less often, less frightening, and more enlightening.

When Light illumines our mind and body, Joy, Growth, Grace, and Ease naturally ascend from within. It is then that we move into our metaphorical House of Wholeness as the Light of Infinite Intelligence floods our Being and cleanses away Fear. This is what the Persian mystic and poet Hafiz meant when he wrote, "Fear is the cheapest room in the house. I would like to see you living in better conditions." He inferred that while Fear may occupy the darkest, dankest, and least desirable room in the metaphorical house of our life, we don't have to share that room. We deserve better accommodations. We can upgrade to our own private room with open windows, plenty of fresh air, and natural light anytime we wish. But, there is a price to do so. The required rent we must pay is the "spiritual coin" of Mindfulness, Wisdom, Faith, Resilience, Diligence, Courage, Time, and Action.

The Importance of Facing Everything and Rethinking

What is needed, rather than running away or controlling or suppressing or any other resistance, is understanding fear; that means watch it, learn about it, come into contact with it. We are to learn about fear, not how to escape it.

J. KRISHNAMURTI

We already know we can't evict or banish Fear from our metaphorical house because that is an impossibility. We also know that we can't outrun Fear because it will shapeshift, run ahead of us, and meet us at our destination. English writer and philologist J.R.R. Tolkien confirmed this dilemma when he wrote: "A man that flies from his fear may find that he has only taken a shortcut to meet it." This is when our acronym **F**ace **E**verything **A**nd **R**ethink comes into play.

We don't have to be surprised, blindsided, or caught off guard when Fear occasionally steps out of its room and pops into our room unannounced. That has been the premise of this book. By being willing to think *proactively* about it, we make space for Fear to share its message with us rather than trying to avoid or anesthetize it because it scares us. Then, we can mindfully listen to it, learn from it, and then send it back to its own room.

We know that coexisting with Fear is not optional if we wish to continue living life as we've known it, but determining how much we allow Fear to frighten us *is*. When we can unflinchingly stand toe-to-toe with our messengers of Fear, we position ourselves to control the narrative. Only then can we lead our dance with Fear rather than allowing it to drag us all around the dance floor.

Let There Be Light:
Looking Behind the Masks

We can easily forgive a child who is afraid of the dark;
the real tragedy of life is when men are afraid of the light.

PLATO

It's said that babies are born with only two intrinsic Fears: the Fear of loud noises and the Fear of falling. This implies that every other Fear we have has been learned or acquired. As Marianne Williamson wrote, "Love is what we are born with. Fear is what we learn." Just as we can't un-think a thought, we can't unlearn that which we have learned because it is information, or experience, embedded in our mind. BUT we can think a NEW thought—a higher thought linked to Love and a remembrance of our oneness.

Fear thrives in the shadows where it tries to loom larger

and scarier than it actually is. The moment we drag our Fears into the Light, they begin to wither up because we can see them for the powerless specters they are. Let us once again affirm that Fear of any kind has only the power we give it, and, therefore, we can revoke that power anytime we choose. *Now is that time.* It's not complicated or difficult. It's as simple as switching on the light in a dark room.

Fear Fears the Light

The black moment is the moment when the real message of transformation is going to come. At the darkest moment comes the light.

JOSEPH CAMPBELL

Fear doesn't like Light. It loses much of its power the moment we drag it out of the darkness and expose it to the luminosity of Truth. In the context of this book, Light signifies the Truth. The ultimate Truth is that God is Light, and, therefore, Infinite Intelligence is the point of origination of Light.

When we remember to call It forward in our Awareness, the Light of Infinite Intelligence illuminates our way through the density and darkness of all Fear. The practice is to remember our oneness with It in the present moment, manifesting as Wisdom, Knowledge, Understanding, Strength, Faith, and Love. In Its highest vibration, God is Love.

While switching on the light in a darkened home may not change where the furniture in each room is located, it enables us to perceive it differently, freeing us to safely walk around it without harming ourselves. In the Light of day, most everything is less frightening. Not only must we "let" there be Light, we must "allow" there to be Light by remembering our oneness with It and making space for It to be revealed.

Light is Wisdom, and Wisdom is simply a collection of past experiences brought to this moment and then applied in a manner that allows It to affect the future in a beneficent way. Yes, *allow* there to be Light!

In this book, we have gathered many valuable and revealing insights through our conversations with the usual suspects, i.e., the Seven Messengers of Fear and their descendants. Fortunately for us, if we ask the right questions, they are very generous with the information we require. And, equally fortunate for us, they are not always the sharpest knives in the drawer. In short, they have betrayed themselves by telling us how to mitigate them, how to put them in their place, and how to defang and tame them by remembering one simple thing: the common link all the minions of Fear share.

The One Common Link

Man cannot possess anything as long as he fears death.
But to him who does not fear it, everything belongs.

LEO TOLSTOY

It's important to remember that, while their numbers are many, the messengers of Fear and their descendants (the usual suspects) are all tethered to one common belief.

Imagine each suspect of Fear standing before us in a lineup. By using deductive reasoning, as if we were the lead detective in a case of mistaken identity, it is possible to see behind the mask that each messenger of Fear and its descendants wears. Can we perceive the one common link between them all that tethers them to the energy of Fear?

Regardless of the disguise it wears, the one thing every Fear has in common is that they're all attached to a concern of death or loss of something or someone. When we remain anchored in this awareness, we are then *empowered* to transcend that fear. With this insight, we can understand that the concern of loss or the death of something or someone is the invisible culprit behind every frightful event, thought, or feeling we experience. Understanding this doesn't always lessen the concern of loss, but it helps us put it in Perspective and see it through the eyes of a benevolent Universe, which is the Source of Life and Light, the Source of All That Is.

As we mindfully peruse this compilation of the Seven Messengers of Fear and their descendants that we've been introduced to, it's not difficult to perceive the invisible concern of loss or death attached to each of them:

Anger
Rage & Resentment

Worry
Anxiety & Regret

Judgement
Superiority, Inferiority & Hate

Selfishness
Greed, Jealousy & Envy

Shame
Guilt, Embarrassment & Perfectionism

Loneliness
Vulnerability & Pride

Uncertainty
Change, Doubt & Procrastination

(NOTE: If we were to consider the many phobias known to plague humankind this list would be endless.)

As we consider this list of Fear's greatest façades, the practice is one of Remembrance, Understanding, Non-Judgement, Compassion, Self-Inquiry, and Action.

When we witness our self, or another, displaying any of the various emotions and actions, the only question we have to ask ourselves is this: "What do I, or what does this person, fear losing at this moment?" When we can answer that question with Discernment and Understanding, it opens the door for a compassionate response rather than a reaction based on the perceived behavior.

Remembering that all Fear is attached to a concern of loss of something creates a portal to a new world of inner Peace. Metaphysically speaking, if we are one with the Source of All That Is, what's to lose? While it may be considered a cavalier statement at first blush, it is true nonetheless. Once we realize our oneness with God (the Universe), we have bridged the gap between cause and effect. To embody the affirmation, "God is, I am," aligns us with First Cause, which encompasses the Source of every need we may have. Fear, in any form, is the "cause" that separates us from an awareness of our oneness with our Source. Understanding the point of origination of our Fear is the only way to deal with it at the level of cause rather than effect.

Since we are continuously becoming cause to our own effect, the quintessential question has to be: "What is it, in this moment, I fear losing?" While the resolution to the question is simple, it may not always be easy because either that which we fear losing is within the sphere of our influence or it isn't. This is a call for the Wisdom to know and understand the difference. Both are fundamental to our Destiny and inner Peace. Remember, the motto "High involvement and low attachment" always seems to be the mark of a wise person.

Let us involve ourselves with participating in Life at a level that transcends Fear and places our focus on that which *is* within the sphere of our influence, rather than what isn't.

Will Fear Be a Friend or Foe?
It's Time to Decide

To overcome fear is the greatest adventure
of the mind of man {humankind}.

ERNEST HOLMES

With a heightened Perspective and a refocused Perception, "overcoming" Fear can be seen as an adventure in which we can determine our own Destiny. Let us not confuse *overcoming* Fear with *defeating* Fear. The word, "overcome" is defined as: "To succeed with dealing with a problem or difficulty." My point is that it's about how we choose to deal with the many-headed beast *proactively* that leads to our success in creating a life worth living despite its occasional appearance.

We are meant to meet, not defeat, our Fears. We are meant to dance with our Fears and allow them to educate us, not frighten us. In writing this book, my intention is to confirm that while Fear is a problem we need to confront and deal with, rather than avoid or run from, there is an exquisite Life that awaits us on the far side of the adventure. Because you have read *When Fear Speaks... Listen* to this point, you already know you deserve that exquisite Life, yes? The question is, "Are you ready to claim it?"

As mentioned throughout, the secret to this quest lies in what mythologist Joseph Campbell referred to as the "Hero's Journey"—our willingness and ability to leave the "Castle" of our comfort zone in search of a more meaningful and rewarding Life despite the Fears and difficulties that lie between us and our triumphant return.

In successfully encountering and befriending our Fears along the way, rather than facing them as ruthless opponents, we return from the quest a better, braver, and more well-developed person. Campbell wrote, "The hero journey is inside of you; tear off the veils and open the mystery of yourself...Perhaps some of us have to go through dark and devious ways before we can find the river of peace or the highroad to the soul's destination."

If we wish to navigate on that *river of peace*, we must each go on our own personal quest, a daring journey that inspires us to leave the confines and comfort of the known. It's only there, on our courageous journey to a more fulfilling Life, that we'll be able to meet our messengers and overcome them. After all, that is why our messengers of Fear are there—for us to transcend and overcome them and prove how much we deserve the rewards that wait beyond them.

We know we were not placed here in this world by accident. We are here "on purpose." We know that we each have a calling, a reason, and a purpose for being: to accomplish that which is uniquely ours to do. Ironically, every Fear that lives within us knows it, too, and is hardwired to run interference if it can. Herein lies the Journey of the Heart, the journey we were born to take.

The highroad to the soul is to venture beyond the confining walls of our own certainties where Fear awaits to teach us just how strong and resilient we are. But, now that we speak and understand the vernacular of Fear, we are equipped to identify and deal with it differently, *responsively* rather than *reactively*.

Now we know we can listen to, learn from, and transcend whatever Fear may attempt to wedge itself between ourselves and the Life of our dreams and aspirations. Doing what is ours to do, then, becomes a rewarding and noble feat.

We are empowered to return from our sojourn with our personal *holy grail* in hand. What I know is that if one person can do it, we all can do it. We are each on the Quest of a Lifetime, and with the Knowledge, Faith, and Courage gained, we shall return home differently than when we departed.

We shall forever be changed as we redefine our relationship with the Seven Messengers of Fear and their many descendants. It's time to decide: "Will Fear be a friend or foe?"

Face **E**verything **A**nd **R**ethink is sage advice. The ultimate question now becomes: "Are we listening?"

I feel blessed knowing that *you* and I are on the journey together.

Peace,

Dennis Merritt Jones

About the Author

Throughout his lifetime, Dennis Merritt Jones, DD, has been on a quest to inspire and lift people to a higher expression of life. His personal vision is to guide people to their purpose, knowing that when one fully awakens to who they are and why they are on the planet, they begin to naturally share their gift with humankind and, in the process, create an enriching life for themselves and the world around them.

As an author, Dennis has written seven books (listed on page 155). He founded the Center for Spiritual Living in Simi Valley, where he served for 23 years, and contributed numerous articles and columns for *Huffington Post, Science of Mind Magazine*, and various local publications. Of his books, *The Art of Abundance, The Art of Uncertainty* and *The Art of Being* were recipients of a Nautilus Award, which highlights books that offer new ideas and options for a better world for everyone. In addition, both writings have received the Books for a Better Life Award from the Multiple Sclerosis Society. *The Art of Uncertainty* was also the 1st runner-up in the 2012 Books for Conscious Living. Study Guides are available for this and other books as a free download at www.DennisMerrittJones.com.

Dennis believes we each have the capacity and, ultimately, the responsibility to contribute something positive to this world, leaving it a better place than it was when we arrived. His teachings promote a contemporary, life-affirming, spiritually logical, and positive outlook on life, which are reflected in his writings. He believes that there is a deeper consciousness of unity, cooperation, and reverence rising in humankind, where the value of all life—regardless of ethnicity, geography, culture, or sexual orientation—will be considered sacred by society's around the world as we approach the challenges of 21st century living.

For more information, please contact
info@DennisMerrittJones.com

Books by
Dennis Merritt Jones, DD

The Art of Uncertainty
How to Live In the Mystery of Life and Love It
978-158542-872-4

The Art of Being
101 Ways to Practice Purpose In Your Life
978-158542-706-2

The Art of Abundance
Ten Rules for a Prosperous Life
978-039918-393-5

Your ReDefining Moments
Becoming Who You Were Born to Be
978-039916-580-1

Encouraging Words
Articles and Essays That Prove Who You Are Matters
978-091784-962-6

How to Speak Science of Mind
A Seeker's Guide to the Basic Concepts and Terms That Define This
Practical Spiritual Lifestyle
978-087516-858-6

When Fear Speaks...Listen
The 7 Messengers of Fear
978-087516-951-4